Fruit Fly Intelligence

Fruit Fly Intelligence

Awareness of our Interconnections with All That Is Leads to an Extraordinary Life!

Paula Marucci

Co-authored by Spirit

Published by Fruit Fly Publishing Inc.

Author: Paula Marucci
Foreword: John Lee MD, Mac, FRCSC
Editor: Susan Crossman, crossmancommunications.com
Cover and Book Design: Kelly Pasholk, yourbookdesigned.com

Paperback ISBN (978-1-7381247-0-1)

E-book ISBN (978-1-7381247-1-8)

To my babies who are all grown up now:
You'll be in my heart, cause I could not ask for more.

XOXO

Disclaimer

The material in this book is not meant to take the place of sound medical, psychological, legal, financial, pharmaceutical, nutritional, or any other qualified professional advice, it is merely a window into my personal perception of the world and journey in this lifetime. Note that there are as many personal perceptions as there are people on the planet; that's a lot of windows!

All decisions you make based on the information provided in this book shall be your sole and exclusive responsibility; please use your best judgement and common sense. Remember, your free will and/or the free will of others may change an outcome, unless Spirit is driving, which was repeatedly the case with me.

Spirit often speaks metaphorically in all areas of our lives, especially through signs, symbols, and synchronicities. In my case, the predominant theme of interconnectedness was emphasized through my relationships with Spirit, others, and so much more; note that I have used fictitious names where appropriate to respect people's privacy while sharing Spirit's fundamental message with you.

x

Contents

Foreword

"Evidence Based Medicine" is a modern-day guiding principle that patient care should be directed by the use of the best available science and current clinical practice. Although this modern approach to medicine makes perfect sense and is currently widely adopted, one must not forget that it applies to a population. For the individual, there may be nuances that the clinician must consider through science, experience, and intuition to determine the best treatment option.

This intuitive approach was what Dr. Wiliam Osler, considered to be the father of modern medicine, referred to as the "Art of Medicine."[1] It is thought that intuition ("gut feeling", "hunch", "my heart") is a complex interaction of experiences, patterns, scientific knowledge, and emotions. It is likely that there are many other significant factors that we still do not understand. If a mother brings her child to the hospital out of concern, regardless of what the initial tests show, her concern needs to be taken seriously. A mother's intuition cannot be ignored. The best doctors have the medical knowledge, evidence, and experience, but will apply it using their "art" to make the care unique to that patient. Traditional medicine often involved touch. This "healing" may be from the release of neurohormones through touch or perhaps an interaction with our "energy" that we have yet to understand. The "art" of healing and the use of touch is not all that different than what Paula describes in her book as sixth sense, source energy, and intuitive guidance.

The intuitive guidance that Paula refers to is much the same as what I applied in my practice. My pre-operative conversations with my patients are not only to review the need and the specifics of the operation, but to also gauge our synchronicity, i.e., "are we on the same wavelength" going into surgery.

My intuition will often guide me to get the patient in sync with me through conversation and sharing of "energy". It is my firm belief that patients generally do better when they and I share the same "energy" and "belief" going into surgery. Although modern medicine has made significant strides, there is still so much more that we do not comprehend. It is with this humility that I approach patient care with a holistic and open-minded view. As a surgeon, precision and science are essential, but I also use intuition and "channeled energy" to guide the tempo of the operation, when to be aggressive, and when to do less.

What Paula describes in this book is not measured in science, but that does not mean it does not exist.

"Just because we don't understand doesn't mean that the explanation doesn't exist."[2]

— MADELEINE L'ENGLE

Our understanding of energy has transformed from Newtonian physics to Einstein's Theory of Relativity and to quantum physics and particle theory. As Paula correctly describes in her book, all matter and being are made of atomic and subatomic particles along with its corresponding gravitational and electromagnetic energies. Could our "soul", "spirit", or "aura" be our own unique "energy DNA" that is within our physical body? If that is the case, it is reasonable to imagine that these energies from individuals will interact with each other. How they interact may be what some call a "connection" or a "meeting of souls." People who consider themselves intuitive may simply be able to sense this interaction in greater detail and amplitude.

What happens to this "energy DNA" when we die, and our physical body is no longer viable? If the conservation of energy principle is true, then this energy must exist somewhere in the universe. Could this be the "spirit energy" that mediums tap into?

I would encourage readers to approach this book with an open mind, but to not try to understand the complex interaction of physical matter, the subconscious, and the energies that exist all around us and in the spiritual realm. Enjoy the easy read and the entertaining real-life experiences that Paula has eloquently narrated in this book, and apply them to your own individual life in a manner that fits with your beliefs and understanding of the world around us. It may make more sense than you think, at least intuitively!

— John Lee MD, Mac, FRCSC

1 Charles S Bryan, T. Jock Murray, Mark E Silverman, eds., "The Quotable Osler." Journal of the Royal Society of Medicine, v. 96 (August 2003), https://www.ncbi.nlm.nih.gov/pmc/articles/PMC539583/#:~:text=He%20believed%20'that%20the%20practice,admired%20by%20students%20and%20colleagues, Accessed November 19, 2023.

2 Madeleine L'Engle, A Wrinkle in Time, (New York: Square Fish, 2007), 46.

Introduction

"Every thought of yours is a real thing—a force."
~ PRENTICE MULFORD (1834–1891)

I was minutes away from a Tim Hortons restaurant in Ontario, Canada, and looking forward to my customary cup of java when suddenly, a street name popped into view that instantly reminded me of a mentor named Wilson. As I continued driving, I turned my head and saw his name on the side of a building; seconds later, I turned my head the other way and saw a license plate that kept him in my thoughts. It was as if an invisible force was speaking to me through modern-day hieroglyphics; I felt like I was in a trance, and I was compelled to notice the string of information—also known as (AKA) signs—as they pulled into view. Those signs foreshadowed something else to come because minutes later, as I stood in the Tim Hortons line waiting to place my order, I received a text from Wilson. It was completely unexpected and undeniably incredible; it was just like one of those moments when you think of someone and then they call, except it felt more like telepathy on steroids!

Months later, while I was sitting in a plenary

session listening to the General Manager (GM) of the company I was working for, I saw Wilson's smile suddenly become superimposed over the GM's mouth. What the heck?! I thought I was losing my mind! But sure enough, Wilson texted during the break. I was utterly gob-smacked! Un-freaking believable!

This is how my awakening to the supernatural realm began, back in 2006, through what I have come to believe was a soulful initiation between *Spirit, Wilson, and me,* (AKA trio bond). It was as if I had been subjected to a bait-and-switch con, and once I was hooked, Spirit installed a new backdrop for my life that would eventually become plastered with events that are stranger than fiction. My trust in Spirit was formed instantaneously as they (I think of Spirit in the plural form) worked to animate my sixth sense (AKA advanced awareness/intuition/ knowing/Extra Sensory Perception) through the other five. This enabled me to see the intangible with my physical eyes, and years later, through my mind's eye. It illuminated a brand-new path which pulled me away from a sixteen-year marriage and inevitably changed the trajectory of my life forever. It would be another seventeen years before I would marry again, and although I wish it could have happened so much sooner, there simply was too much learning in store for me with Spirit; and you are the beneficiary of those lessons.

I liken the experience of my spiritual journey to that of someone who has had a near-death experience (NDE), where they gain the ability to observe themselves and their environment from an ethereally enlightened perspective, then wake up from the event so much wiser than before. I am sure you've heard many stories about how vibrantly colorful their surroundings were during the NDE. Thankfully, I didn't have to go through a near death for my great awakening to take place; instead, it was kicked off through an initiation which had been tailor-made for me. The chain of events that followed for almost two decades morphed me into an energy channeler.

You may be thinking that twenty years is a long time to go through a series of spiritual lessons, and that an NDE would be a whole lot quicker, right? I completely agree, but I was destined in this lifetime to go through ordinary experiences, imbued with spiritual overtones, which would shapeshift my life into extraordinary realities; and share them with you. Let me explain it in this way: my initiation was like drinking a glass of water, which is an ordinary earthly experience, right? Then, you hear about Dr.

Masaru Emoto's work with water crystals[1] and that's it, your mind is blown! Like a spaceship to the sky! The ordinary experience becomes extraordinary; and if you're anything like me, you will never see a glass of water in quite the same way again. Respect and gratitude are the way in which I interact with water now. Domo arigato Emoto-san.

The new path laid out for me would become filled with constant change and plenty of surges of internal energy that I refer to as a supercharged-quickening feeling; this is my phrase for the feeling I get when Spirit is moving through me. Over the course of many years, Spirit enhanced my other physical senses as well, but in the end it was my visual, auditory, and tactile senses that were upgraded the most. These tweaks enable me to fall into a spiritually induced trance within seconds, and this altered state, while I am gushing with gratitude, enhances my sixth sense. From my perspective, the sixth sense can sound as powerfully gripping as a marching band trampling through your brain. Therefore, the penultimate reason for sharing my journey of personal transformation is to help others release fear and become inspired to embrace the sixth sense as their personal navigating system (PNS). This system has our best interests at heart; it increases our vitality, which attracts more joy; and it can become one's *Source* of truth. Your PNS can take you on a beautiful ride, like an NDE filled with vibrant colors and unimaginable landscapes; and I trust that this book will take you on a beautiful ride too.

Spirit sharpened my sixth sense through signs, symbols, and synchronicities that were tied to a variety of relationships for my soul's growth. It was a direct way for Spirit to get my attention because relationships are an integral part of the human experience. But Spirit took it to a whole new level by showing me how we can relate with *everything*. Therefore, the apex purpose of this book for you, dear reader, is to share that:

> *The relationships we cultivate in our lives with all that exists in the physical and non-physical realms bring more value than the eyes can see; for we are dynamically interconnected beings that vibrate with the life force of Source energy; knowing this leads to an extraordinary life!*

I hope that *Fruit Fly Intelligence* encourages you to pause and reflect on your own relationships through an expanded lens, so that you may see the intangible value inherent within each of them, and possibly a soul-contracted life lesson or two. However, it is heartbreak that is most notably one of the greatest catalysts for the soul's evolution. Here is a rather staggering fact about heartbreak in the world of my beloved fruit flies: this study found that males turned to "the bottle" when they were rejected by potential mates. [2] It fascinates me how similar they are to humans, regardless of gender of course. Indeed, heartbreak of any kind can have a profound influence on our emotions and subsequent behaviors; therefore, it would be advantageous for you to reflect on how your own heartbreaking experiences have been important for your soul's growth. One of the byproducts of this growth is the ability to view your world more expansively, which can light you up in the most celestial way.

I realize now that my initiation gave me a front-row seat into the supernatural realm, and it is where I've been sitting for nearly two decades, with Spirit in the driver's seat; and as a result, my vitality has soared. But it wasn't all rainbows and butterflies. Although many changes were necessary for my growth to occur, it was often painful and confusing for me, my children, and others in my life. I would ultimately come to understand that Wilson had been hand-picked by Spirit to be an emotional resuscitator of sorts, by activating my heart center, not in a romantic way, but in a way that caused me to wake up from old programming to see the magic in life all around us. Wilson was the first "breadcrumb," if you will, that Spirit used to lure me forward, and they know how much I love bread! We were placed together under the earthly guise of a mentoring relationship, however, the labels we use to describe human connections are irrelevant to Spirit, unless it is meaningful for your soul to grow. Spirit used this initiation to shift my sense of who I was and what was possible, and guided me into a new phase of growth that was no less than astounding! I have heard other people use the term "soul activator", which seems like an appropriate description of Wilson's role in my initiation. Everyone will have these sorts of encounters at some point in their lives; however, our judgements can limit our ability to use them as a springboard for growth. Because of the constellation of signs that prefaced Wilson's communication with me, I knew I was not alone, and I referred to the invisible forces behind them, collectively, as Spirit.

A Spiritual Foundation

The foundation of this book is spiritual in nature and completely devoid of religious views, so please insert the word(s) which best suit your belief system; the acronym BYOG applies here, and it stands for "Bring Your Own God." Please know that my intention is not to sell you on my belief system—there simply is no need for that—but rather to share how Spirit blew its cosmic breath through my soul to awaken its earthly purpose for this lifetime, and for the world to find more joy here on this beautiful planet. Going forward, you may see me interchange the terms: Source, Universe, Creator, Divine, Infinite Field of Consciousness, God, Spirit Guides, Guides, and my Love Team (in spirit) because for me, "they," rather than a "him," "her," or "it," are different expressions of the whole. However, you will see that I reference the term Spirit the most, and I define them as animated realities of Source energy. This might be an unusual concept for some people. Most of us have come to see a higher power as a singular being who knows all, sees all, and is capable of anything.

Anyway, after this initiation into the realm of the supernatural, extreme telepathic and synchronistic events continued to show up regularly in all areas of my life, and my engagement was effortless. I eagerly connected the dots to uncover messages Spirit was sending my way. I couldn't get enough, so I began reading books I was drawn to with the hope of finding answers to these mysterious occurrences. When

I was ready, Spirit pushed me to write a book of my own. My life became extraordinary once I understood how the Universe speaks through all that is, especially through our relationships, I began listening, accepting, and trusting with every fiber of my being; Spirit became my source of truth.

In *Fruit Fly Intelligence*, I delve into the awakening and expansion of my right intuitive brain capabilities which were ushered in through my left logical and rather skeptical mind. This unexpected development created a tsunami of emotions which drove a massive paradigm shift within, as my old world began to crumble and then rebuilt itself in the most unrecognizable way. The process required me to question long-held morals and beliefs; and with that, I came to accept that there is more than one way to live a life beyond one's old programming, no matter how well intended it may have been. For me, it was an experience like Roger Bannister's four-minute mile[3], which busted through the beliefs of his time.

However, in my case, it felt more like the Universe had slipped multi-dimensional virtual-reality goggles over my eyes, and once I was able to see my environment dressed in this new cosmic reality, I would never be able to see and experience life in the same way again. Quite frankly, I didn't want to. I

became aware that there is so much more to life beyond our five senses, but sadly, our beliefs and judgements erect barriers to our own conscious expansion
and subsequent contribution to the world. It took me
years to reach this conclusion, and I'm still finding
new layers of meaning around it even today.

Prior to the telepathic synchronicities that preced-
ed the text Wilson sent me in the coffee shop that day
so long ago, I had been grappling with a deep feeling
of emptiness which had led to a growing dissatisfac-
tion with my life. I was unable to comprehend why
I felt this way. From the outside, it looked like I was
on par with the average middle-class Canadian family: I was married, and my husband and I had two
beautiful children, respectable jobs, a home, cars,
and so on. It was puzzling because I was not even
sure what I was yearning for, I just felt an emptiness,
like a flat line in my emotions. I would have opted
for anything that made me feel more alive. Was that
it? Was I emotionally dead? And if so, when had that
happened? I loved my family as well as our friends,
and I absolutely adored my children. It turned out
that those feelings ran deep and intersected with my
life purpose. In hindsight, I realized that Spirit had
ignited those feelings to spark an awakening process.
This had increased my conscious desire to search for

greater meaning in my life and then help others find greater meaning in their lives, as well.

And then, ode to a life-changing event, I had what is called a "tower moment" in tarot-speak, in the form of my divorce. A tower moment is an event that rattles you out of your slumber and wakes you just enough to take the wheel, even if you have no idea where you are headed. During this time, I remember whispering a mantra to myself about not wanting to live my life in black and white, I wanted to live in color. Well, I discovered that my internal words had legs! Voicing those words aloud and mentioning divorce to my then-husband resulted in a personal transition from feeling an emptiness, to feeling the sting of emotional turmoil as I realized the earthly consequence of the decision I had made. My decision caused pain for my husband, my children, my family, and friends. The suffering I had created was not lost on me at all; and so, I sought solace by turning inward, as many people do. I am sure you will agree that emotional pain can lead to remarkable growth and expansion if you let it (your soul craves this); that was the case with me, especially once Spirit illuminated the reason for my departure from the marriage. I will give you a hint, it involves a steep supernatural learning curve about my life purpose and what I was meant to contribute to the world.

In hindsight, I was able to see that divorce was necessary because my identity had been swallowed up in old programming that filtered through the roles, routines, and responsibilities of my daily life; and I needed the space to grow. I had been on autopilot, hence the empty feeling, and at the time I thought, *aren't we all*? But after my world started to fall apart, stranger than fiction began to take up residence and became the backdrop of my life. My Spirit Guides wanted to get my attention, and indeed they did, through increasingly explicit signs, symbols, and synchronicities. Given that you are here reading about my journey, I suspect that your Spirit Guides are trying to do the same with you.

Signs, Symbols, and Synchronicities

From a non-scientific perspective and my own point of view, I have come to believe that signs, symbols, and synchronicities are fueled by an invisible energy which teleports them into the earthly realm. They typically come to me in a pop-art-like fashion, and once received, I am not able to unsee, unhear, untaste, unsmell, unfeel, or unknow them. This invisible energy is all around us all the time, and we tap into it on a constant basis; we are *it* and *it* is us! Sound far-fetched? Well, imagine a wall outlet in your home. The electrical current it makes available is not visible to the naked eye, and yet, when we plug something into the socket, we get a result: our hair dries, water boils, the dishwasher cleans our dishes, and so forth. My point is this: just because you cannot see something, does not mean it cannot be there.

At some point along my path, the Universe had uploaded a superpower of sorts into my being, and once zapped I was forced to emerge, with the caveat that I would share my evolution with like and not-so-like-minded individuals around the world. I was yanked directly into vibrational alignment with the Infinite Field of Consciousness (AKA Source energy); *pssst!* that's where the fruit fly comes in. I knew that whatever my assignment was going forward, my role would be unlike anything I had ever experienced in this lifetime before. The old Paula craved the life of a wallflower and opted to shapeshift seamlessly into the background of life; however, the updated version was pushed forward by Spirit, as if coaxed onto the stage by a grown-up.

Although it took a minute—okay, more like a couple of decades—for this upgrade to fully reveal itself, I knew that this way of seeing the world had always been a part of me, as if I had been tethered to this cosmic wisdom through my belly button, that bull-seye where the etheric meets flesh. My unexpected metamorphosis demanded that I find a way to infuse my new perspective into everyday life. But how does one master the art of living every day in the twenty-first century through a shiny new mystical lens? Should I move into this new reality full throttle, or do I tiptoe gingerly, so nobody will notice? I attempted the latter, but Spirit had other plans. Today, I feel more alive and invigorated by the world around me than ever before. Bit by bit along the way, I have developed capabilities that I had never even dreamed of for myself, yet here I am, standing in as an energy channeler and somewhat of an ambassador for the spirit realm to foster communication with the unseen world, work with its magical energy, and help others heal and live an extraordinary life!

While on this journey, I have been privy to an unthinkable range of realities which oscillate between visible and invisible dimensions. Seeing loved ones who have crossed over is a staggering thing, but imagine feeling Spirit poke your physical body to get a point across or seeing aliens on two separate occasions while living in an unassuming fourth-floor condo. It's tempting to dismiss someone who says they've had this kind of experience as being a few bricks short of a load, and that's exactly what I would have done a few decades earlier too, before my nice tidy picket-fence life started unraveling and re-forming as some sort of fascinating multi-dimensional adventure story. Because of Spirit, I have been able to deliver future predictions, provide messages from loved ones who have crossed over, and diminish people's pain and other stressors by hovering my hands over them. I didn't ask to be given these experiences, and at first, I was somewhat uncomfortable telling people about them. I initially greeted the idea that I could ease people's pain and talk to their departed loved ones with a skeptical eye. *Yeah. Right. Sure, Paula. You're imagining things again*, I thought. Was I losing it?! And let's face it, there are charlatans all over the world who give authentic channelers a bad name. But as time went on, more and more people validated my accuracy levels: departed souls were sharing granular details for their loved ones here on earth; like providing their pet name for a family member, and determining the exact location of a bodily issue, and naming specifics in various situations that had previously been confusing for people. It's hard to believe you're cuckoo when you're consistently coming up with correct information. Eventually, I started to fully embrace it myself. I've included some testimonials in this book to help you come to terms with all this too. Especially if you have started to get those high-vibrational intuitive hits that are shifting how you see the reality of your life.

Today, I recognize this is simply my new life, and one that I treasure deeply and will never take lightly. Now, I fully understand that Spirit channels through everything; even a seemingly insignificant little fruit fly; hence the title of this book, chosen by Spirit. Their hope is that people come to realize and respect that all things vibrate with the life force of Source energy.

With Spirit at the helm, I have been astounded for almost two decades by the expansion of my reality. I'm so grateful for this gift and my pure connection to Spirit. I have finally found my place in this world, and it has nothing to do with an address: the feeling of *home* comes from within.

Although I have not been certified to use the title psychic medium, and I truly don't feel right proclaiming myself as such, it's a phrase that most people will understand when I'm speaking about my ability to communicate with the invisible realm; however, this term doesn't cover the breadth and depth of the mystical experiences which I have had to date; and I know that I'm not special in this department. Everyone has likely had a peculiar event or two in their lives. My peek behind the so-called "veil" is not a new phenomenon: people have secretly sought wisdom and foresight from oracles likely since the beginning of humanity. However, I learned of one bonafide oracle by the name of Mary Hayes Chynoweth (1825-1905) who had an extraordinary entity tell her that "...she would spend the remainder of her life healing others." In one article she was dubbed a "Psychic Healer."[4] We exist. Perhaps you are one too.

Cozy up on the Couch

In this book, I will share situations that I have experienced, lessons I have learned, messages I have channeled from Spirit, testimonials I have gratefully received, and quotes from wise souls. Even more riveting are the incredible images I have captured along the way which highlight some of those moments when Spirit was attempting to get my attention. And by the way, Spirit is attempting to get your attention too. So, grab a coffee or your favorite glass of wine and cozy up on the couch for a trip that may make you raise an eyebrow or two. Oh, and don't waste your time thinking that I'm crazy because I beat you to it, although Spirit has proven otherwise time and time and time again.

This book may read like a fictional novel at times, with a dash of sci-fi sprinkled in, but I can assure you that it is not! It's simply the details of a life lived with the increasing awareness that there is something *out there*, that is actually *right here*, and it can guide us to less stress and anxiety and more hopefulness and fulfillment. My wish in sharing my journey is to encourage you to start watching and listening for Spirit's attempts to get your attention, so that you can find more meaningful moments in your life and vibrate with joy on a daily basis. We're not nuts. This stuff is real! In *Fruit Fly Intelligence,* you will see how an expanded perception of the ordinary can lead to an extraordinary life! And I hope that this book, co-authored by Spirit, will become a valuable resource for those of you seeking to experience a closer connection with the invisible realm too. Now, I will share with you how I became consciously aware of my connection to Spirit and how my journey beyond the so-called "veil" unfolded...bottom line, be discerning and buckle up! Let's jump in!

1

Every Child is Precious

"How does the meadow-flower its bloom unfold?
Because the lovely little flower is free down to
its root, and, in that freedom bold..."

~ WILLIAM WORDSWORTH (1770–1850)

"She's coming," shouted Lynda on her *un*expected date of confinement. It was April 27, 1968, when I made my grand entrance—two months early and, according to the beliefs of the time, shamefully out of wedlock—into the world of my young, blue-collar parents. At around the age of five, I had a febrile seizure which occurred seemingly out of the blue. I had to be rushed to the hospital and required yearly electroencephalograms (EEG) to make sure I didn't suffer any long-term effects. The doctor called it a febrile seizure, and Spirit called it an "outage," either way, I was down for the count; thankfully there were no further incidents. As a child, I was rather quiet, shy, and odd really. Up until my tweens, I could be seen twirling on the spot anywhere in the home; somehow it relaxed me. When my family members saw me spinning like a skater corkscrewing into the floor, they would whisper amongst themselves; I can only imagine what I would be labeled today if I were a youngster seen doing that. I suspect I would have been placed on the spectrum, which is neither here nor there, it would be their label, not mine. During my childhood, my father often said that children should be seen and not heard; so, I guess my twirling satisfied his request. Overall, my formative years were uneventful from a paranormal perspective, except for one woo-woo event which occurred at some point before third grade. My younger sister and I shared a bedroom in our Hamilton apartment, and we both remember seeing the hand of a man in the closet, and *he* was sliding our clothes on hangers very slowly across the rack. To this day, I am not able to fall asleep with the closet door open, especially given what I do now. Although I can only recall this one paranormal experience, I suspect that I may have had an imaginary friend or two during my childhood, because as a grownup who channels energy, I have come to understand that a doorway to communication with Spirit is through our imagination, and we are all born with this ability.

In those early years of my life, it was discovered

that I had some comprehension issues, challenges pronouncing the letter "s," and mild hearing loss, to boot. Because of all this, I had to step out of the classroom twice a week to get some one-to-one assistance. Ultimately, I knew that I was different, and not in an endearing way. Etched in my memory is an experience that made me feel even more unsettled at school. I didn't fit in with my Grade 3 classmates, and thanks to my teacher, (AKA Mrs. Meanie), my parents were informed of something I had done in class at the behest of a fellow student. He dared me to grab a crayon, get up in front of a seated class, walk over to the pencil sharpener that was bolted onto the windowsill, and sharpen the crayon. So, I did. Well, Mrs. Meanie snapped at me and ordered me to sit back down. A parent-teacher meeting ensued. The teacher's behavior after that made me feel even more like an outcast. On a sidenote, we know that creation begins with an idea of the mind and crayon sharpeners are now available; 'nuff said! In short, Mrs. Meanie didn't do me any favors, wish she could see me now, Snap! If you have a Mrs. Meanie in your past, I invite you to stop letting her take up space in your head and your heart. You're worth more than that.

One of my fondest grade-school memories involves Mrs. C., and it still puts a smile on my face to this day. I started figure skating lessons when I was nine, and I was taking them more frequently by Grade 7; Mrs. C. was aware of this. So, on one winter afternoon, a group of us seventh graders were making our way from one icy portable to another without coats on. As we waited on the steps for Mrs. C. to unlock the door and let us in, she chastised the group for being improperly dressed for the wintry weather. Once we were inside and all seated, she called me back to her desk and said, "Why were you outside without a coat, you should know better, you're an athlete!" Whether she was trying to help an awkward kid, or she was being completely sincere about her thought of me as an athlete, her words reverberated through me and warmed my heart.

Given my entrance into the world, my shy personality, and the household I grew up in, I found myself displaying some strange obsessive/compulsive behaviors, commonly labelled as OCD, in my childhood years. My behaviors were perpetuated by a constant anxious drone that I felt within. As a child, I coped by doing more twirling, but as I got older, I began to go inward to pray, and I frequently craved the quiet hum of a church. Back then, I would randomly start my day alone sitting in a pew and later, as a teenager, headed to the high school chapel during lunch hour for some quiet time. At some point during my tween years, I had a creative inspiration to write a little poem that reflected my unsettled state, so I thought I would share it with you. It goes like this:

Life is a circle it travels around.
Leaving yourself where you're nowhere to be found.
In loneliness and horror and ever so more,
Life is a circle for you to explore.

Unfortunately, my parents separated just a few weeks shy of my sixteenth birthday; that gave me plenty of reasons to start exploring. Back in the 1980s, divorce was less common and therefore carried a negative stigma which made me feel even more abnormal and "less than" the kids whose parents were still together. The ongoing feeling of emotional instability caused a dis-ease in the family home. In hindsight, I could see that my father's less-than-desirable tendencies and my mother's routine display of frustration and unhappiness had a lasting impact on the family, as well as on my self-esteem; this led to a perpetual dance with fear which I remained tethered to for decades. Please know that I am not blaming my parents at all, on the contrary, I understand that people are complex beings; so when we spend time with just one person, like a family member, a friend, a neighbor, a stranger, and so forth, it can lead to all sorts of conflicts, confusion, disillusionment, and judgements; as well as a range of low vibrational emotions, like shame, guilt, apathy, grief, fear, anger, jealousy, and so on; those emotions can impact the decisions we make.

It is common to lose oneself when bumping up against the whole of another person; and by this I am referring to their physical, emotional, mental, and spiritual self. I believe that many of the relationships we find ourselves in are destined connections that we choose before each lifetime to foster our soul's growth; and these are the challenging connections that can wake us up to higher vibrational living.

Straight into Independence

Ultimately, I am grateful because my parents' divorce forced me to begin the process of uncovering who Paula truly is. Shortly after my father moved out of our home, I was hired to work at a local Swiss Chalet restaurant. The family upheaval led me right out of stagnancy and straight into independence. I see each experience since then, no matter how small, as a steppingstone which has helped to create a solid foundation within; and I am fiercely independent to this day. I never thanked my father for leaving and, at the time, it was incredibly painful for our family, but I am glad he did. Dad, thanks for playing a part in my soul's journey and then stepping aside so that I could soar! Oh, and Mom, thanks for taking such good care of me all those years as you were wrestling with your new identity as a single mother.

Fortunately, my skating lessons continued. As a young figure skater, I knew that I was just average at best, but somehow, my beloved skating coach, Harriet Lyons, saw something more and encouraged me to try out for a local Christmas ice show, which was being choreographed by internationally recognized choreographer, Brian Foley. Luckily, I was hired to perform in that show for two years in a row.

I had another moving experience in my late teens when members of the skating club, along with my coach, Harriet, encouraged me to participate in a local festival pageant. The chosen "Queen" would represent the pageant and be its ambassador for a year. I felt absolutely petrified to do so, but with a shot of peach schnapps in my belly, I did it anyway and was completely shocked when the big day came and one of the competitors shouted, "Paula, you won!" I was stunned! Although this was a relatively small event, it gave me my first inkling that I might be able to speak in front of a large crowd—and even more shocking was the sound of the applause I received from the audience. A few weeks later, I was touched when I saw a picture of my beautiful Italian grandmother captured in the background of a newspaper article that highlighted my win. After she passed away in 2004, I received messages from two different psychic mediums indicating that she was coming through to speak with me. It warms my heart because we didn't share that kind of bond when she was alive; I often hear the song "Melody of Love" by Bobby Vinton playing in my head, which is her signature telepathic move.

In 1987, at the age of nineteen and yet again with the encouragement of my coach, Harriet, I was hired by an American producer to skate in an international ice show. Three decades later, I am still incredibly grateful for the honor and privilege of performing at the New Fujiya Hotel in Atami, Japan. Imagine an ordinary girl taking her first commercial flight ever to Las Vegas for rehearsals! We were there for about two-and-a-half weeks. On one occasion, I remember watching the famous American pair skating team, Tai Babilonia and Randy Gardner, practice prior to our turn on the ice. It was thrilling!

The American Super Dream cast flew to Japan on Christmas Day, 1987, and we lived there for almost six months. I turned the big 2-0 while I was there in April 1988. One of my favorite memories of this ice show was the time the cast performed for a large corporate dinner event. The room was filled with hundreds of Japanese men wearing yukatas (robes) and Geishas looking poised and beautiful; the setting was buzzing with a happy, peaceful, yet professional vibe; it was absolutely exhilarating! It was wonderous for me to step into this rich culture, with its neon lights, Buddhist temples and Shinto shrines, the alluring Japanese language, and the vibration of the taiko drum. Those sights, sounds, smells, tastes, and feels are all near and dear to my heart even now. It felt incredible wearing colorful costumes in gorgeous fabrics and feathers as I performed on the ice. I was acclimating to a life filled with G-strings, and enjoyed lively figure skating parties, all for the first time. It was an experience you simply cannot get from a textbook.

Bitten by the Ice Show Bug...Again

After my return from this incredibly life-changing event, I found it difficult to leave behind that colorful reality and settle into a more mundane routine.

I eventually found my stride once I became a Registered Nurse, however, in 1995, at the age of twenty-seven, I was bitten by the ice show bug again, and felt totally blessed to be hired by the same producer to perform in a summer show for seven weeks at Mitsui Greenland in Kumamoto, Japan; I was hired again the following year for a five-week stint at the same location. These experiences were transformative indeed, and I couldn't be more grateful to those earth angels: my mother, my beloved coach, Harriet Lyons (R.I.P.—and PS I know you can hear me), and the American producer who hired me for those three shows.

I had to summon up a lot of courage to take this giant leap into the unknown, venturing beyond the borders of Canada, and I'm sure glad I did! As a sidenote, other people can be instrumental in helping us identify important contacts we are meant to make, places we are meant to go, and actions we are meant to take; however, it is incumbent upon each of us to be awake and aware enough to heed their advice.

One of the items that was to become a touchstone of comfort for me during this time and long thereafter was a Sandicast cat, which I purchased from a beloved Japanese friend's gift shop in September 1996. About this time, I also bought a beautiful Precious Moments keepsake—an indigenous girl who is wearing a feathered head-dress with pink hearts around the headband; her hair is fastened into two little braids. She is wearing a beaded necklace and a long, warm, neutral-toned dress with adorable little moccasins peeking through the bottom fringe. She is holding her left arm up at a 90-degree angle with her palm facing the world, and in her right hand she is gripping a flower; on the bottom are the words, "Bless-Um You." Although today this phrase may seem culturally insensitive, at the time I thought it was a form of well-wishing to another which I felt drawn to because it was sweet and peaceful. I have a photograph of myself sitting on the steps of my earliest childhood home on Rosewood Road which kind of looks like this young porcelain girl, and to this day she is near and dear to my heart.

Reflection:

I would answer William Wordsworth's question about the meadow-flower that appears at the start of this chapter in this way: every child is precious because we are tethered to the light of Source energy; because it shines, we shine too. Somehow little Paula knew to ask for guidance and grabbed the hands that reached out to her while she walked through life.

Over time, my relationship with Source has shifted from a religious-based view to a more solitary concept, as I was drawn inward to connect directly with God, the term I used at the time; by doing so, I felt a greater sense of inner peace that I hadn't felt before.

Looking back on my early years, I can see that I have displayed a life-long tendency toward solitude. I now understand that it was critical to get to know myself and learn the language of the Universe. When I stumbled onto numerology, it endorsed my tendency toward solitariness as well. Now as a channeler, I understand that we are all connected with Source, and harnessing its energy, richly available within signs, symbols, and synchronicities, is key to living an extraordinary life! I encourage you to ask whomever you pray to for assistance on your path. There will be highs and lows, of course, but the highs will be better than you could ever imagine. I am truly grateful to have been offered so many incredible opportunities early on in my life; it has allowed me to bloom in unexpected ways.

2

My Deconstructed Self

*"The art of life lies in a constant readjustment
to our surroundings."*

~ OKAKURA KAKUZO (1863–1913)

I felt helpless and alone standing in front of a patient who had bled out all over the floor, and even
though I had chosen to become a nurse in my early
twenties, it was hard to face the traumas many of my
patients endured. Sadly, facing death was a part of
the job description. At the age of twenty-two, just
three years before my nursing career began, I married a man I had been dating for five years. I was a
little too young by today's standards, but I was in
hot pursuit of societal goals back then. It took about
ten years for the demands of my nursing career and
life beyond the walls of a hospital before I developed
feelings of restlessness. At that point I instinctively
began to search for more, as the feeling permeat-
ed my daily existence and induced a constant burn
within. During that time I was fully engaged in my

nursing career and worked in Acute Care Medicine, Surgical Post-Op, Endoscopy, Intensive Care, and Emergency at three small community hospitals, and I often found myself filled with anxiety. I poured my heart and soul into caring for patients who were dealing with all sorts of acute and chronic illnesses such as multiple sclerosis, cancer, mental illness, gastrointestinal bleeds, acquired immunodeficiency syndrome (AIDS), chronic obstructive pulmonary disease (COPD), dementia, and so much more.

I tenderly remember specific patients who I attempted to help through endless challenges; some of their stories were gut wrenching. I'm sure that every nurse has memories that have left indelible marks on their heart. Three of my patients nearly broke my heart in two because of what they were dealing with. To make matters even worse, I found the twelve-hour shifts absolutely brutal to get through, and doing three in a row was completely draining, depressing, and soul-sapping. I felt that the nursing attire for most of my career should have come with a pair of roller skates so I could keep up with the demands of the job, and I tended to skip meals just to get things done. I developed the not-so-healthy habit of drinking bottomless cups of coffee to get me through the day and night shifts. The unhealthy patterns I devel-

oped over time led to a self-diagnosis of hypoglyce-
mia, which simply means that I had too little sugar
in my blood, and I needed that fuel to take care of
my patients. I can remember testing my blood sugar
(non-diabetic) one afternoon and discovering that I
was indeed hypoglycemic at 3.6 mmol/L. During
those sugar lows, I experienced a voracious appetite
that would send me zipping through the unit like
the Tasmanian Devil in search of food. During that
period of my life, I would occasionally experience
tingling around the mouth, slurred speech, and extreme lethargy, but despite those symptoms showing
up at work and at home, I made no changes.

Here's what I learned many years later: errat-
ic work schedules, fragmented sleep patterns, sleep
deprivation, inadequate nutrition, chronic constipa-
tion, and the steady jolt of caffeine coursing through
the system can do a real number on the physical
body. That was definitely the case with me; it especially impacted my emotional and mental clarity. I
was not aware of the damage I was causing myself
and, unfortunately, no one showed me the error of
my ways. Now that I understand how our body can
speak to us, thanks to lessons from Spirit, I can see
that mine was screaming out through those symptoms—and yet, I wasn't aware enough to do better.

During work hours when my anxiety amped up, I had the distinct pleasure of experiencing white coat syndrome, where just the sight of a doctor in a lab coat could spike my blood pressure and accelerate my heart rate. This would rear its ugly head at the most inopportune times, which was not ideal when you work amidst a sea of doctors.

I can remember being in a hyper-anxious state one afternoon and overhearing one of the doctors saying to another "is she for real?" Today I would have replied, "yes, goof, I am!" In all fairness though, he was seeing a woman who was frazzled and not at all self-aware. I was still heavily influenced by societal norms, expectations, and people's opinions back then. But it wasn't all bad, I also had the opportunity to work alongside some wonderful doctors, nurses, patients, and family members; I even met a world-renowned singer, a children's television entertainer, and the mother of an international actor, which was refreshing given the environment we were in.

In 1999, I had the incredible privilege of being pregnant with my beautiful baby boy, but as my belly swelled, so too did the fear of "Y2K."[5] Everyone watched and waited for the experts to solve what could have turned out to be a massive computer crisis as the calendar ticked over to January 1, 2000.

Thankfully, all was fine. On March 19, 2000, and at the age of thirty-two, I gave birth to my sweet little boy; and in my experience, there is nothing more precious than motherhood.

During this first pregnancy, I remember stressing about what life would be like for my son in the new millennium. I contemplated what people would look like and eventually understood that the re-emergence of blue- and purple-colored hairstyles, for example, was analogous to our evolving collective consciousness. It is my belief as a channeler that adding color to our lives helps us become more plugged into Source energy. Those of you who understand the chakra system, its colors, and corresponding organs, will appreciate my hair reference; and for those who would like more information, I recommend that you check out Caroline Myss' incredible work on her website: https://www.myss.com/chakras/.[6]

How Will People Behave?

Another worry I had as an expectant mother was about how people would behave moving into this new era; for example, would the pulse on the street feel more accepting and loving, or judgmental and hateful? Tragically, the latter played out on September 11th, 2001, as the world watched when almost three thousand people lost their lives through a horrific terrorist attack on the United States. While the pain of this unthinkable act reverberated around the world, so too did the global conversation, which resulted in swift changes to thwart further attacks. As a mother I dragged those fears—and a host of others—around with me until about six years later, when my initiation into the supernatural realm occurred, with *Spirit, Wilson, and me.* As a result, my personal perception of the world changed forever. However, it wasn't until years later, when I began channeling energy on a more frequent basis and speaking with my clients, that I truly started to comprehend the visual and behavioral shift of humanity; we're simply waking up!

It is refreshing to observe people blending many aspects of their lives and hearing them speak about vision boards to manifest their desires, and clearing their environments of stagnant energy, for example. These behaviors create new experiences for our five senses while tickling the sixth, resulting in an expanded version of humanity, like the unfoldment of a lotus flower that is reaching toward the sun.

Let me expound on this further: I can see that our more open and conscious approach to living is positively impacting the global pulse. We are embracing the fusion of ethnicities, religions, cultures, foods, musical styles, sexual orientations and reorientations, relationship statuses and so much more. These experiences are stirring the collective consciousness, busting our subsequent conversations wide open, and, thankfully, putting our autopilots out of work. I believe this will lead to a more Divine expression of humanity. Fusion ought to be applauded for being a driver for change; separation is not the answer, for it is the coming together in pure love that leads to a positive outcome. People are no longer waiting for permission to express their authentic light, and I love that! Yes, indeed, humanity has evolved and will continue to do so. Pushing our collective mindset outside of its binary boundaries is both liberating and necessary in my view, given that we are birthing more radiant beings into the world.

As an aside, I wish all children were taught how to value people for who they truly are so that we may co-exist peacefully in the sandbox of life; this approach could have a positive and everlasting impact on a global scale. Why don't we teach children to embrace one another, our differences, and our varying points of view (windows of perception), so we can transcend barriers together? If it takes a village to raise a child, then have members of the village failed us? I believe that living authentically fosters a sense of wholeness; and one of its purest byproducts is love. As a channeler, I have come to understand that humans are merely one way that Source express-es itself, and all things are an expression of Source energy; it's God on the move in constant creation.

So, with a dash of courage, curiosity, color, and time, we will create a world that is unlike anything we have ever known before. Yes, modern technol-ogies like Artificial Intelligence (AI) are here, and it will no doubt have a profound effect on our lives; however, AI is just another expression of Source's infinite potential. We are here on the earth plane to experience life fully, which means we may expe-rience things that are good, bad, and/or anything in between. The good news is that we are highly adapt-able, and when we go inward to ask for guidance toward our North Star, we will not only find our life purpose, but we will also be accompanied toward solutions that will improve our lives.

Your Guides can light the way to an extraordi-nary life, despite what is happening around you. There are countless stories about people overcoming unbelievable obstacles, and yet, many say it was the best thing that could have happened to them; a shift occurs that transcends pain and promotes peace. The best part is that your Guides will plug you directly into Source energy where you can see the world from a magical vantage point.

Months after my son was born, I developed an irrational fear that my new baby boy would be taken in the middle of the night by aliens. It's not funny! However, I figured my fears were due to the storm of hormones coursing through my post-partum body. Thankfully, nothing odd happened during that time, at least not that I am aware of, but knowing what I know now as an energy channeler, it's not so far-fetched; and as a mother, I understand that my son has a spiritual calling which is not dissimilar to his mama's. It seems appropriate to share my view that the evolution of humanity will prepare us to inter-act more readily with other beings; and this includes extraterrestrials (aliens). Consider the mention of unidentified aerial phenomena by the United States Department of Defense[7] on April 27, 2020; it hints at the notion that my belief about an alien presence may be accurate.

I understand the gravity of my words, however this is my perspective after having two quite pleasant, yet fleeting encounters with aliens myself. (More about those later.) Simply put, our expansion will help us evolve into a more advanced civilization.

My beautiful daughter was born on September 26, 2002, and from a channeling perspective, I can say that my grown children are living in one of the best eras on our historical timeline; my pre-motherly worries were all for naught, and I couldn't be more thrilled. Please don't misconstrue what I am saying: I realize that life is not that pleasurable for many inhabiting the earth, which sadly reflects the shadowy side of humanity, but I believe that if we become the best version of ourselves while sending love and healing energy to all who are suffering, we can change the world for the better.

An Inner Restlessness

Despite the bliss of motherhood, I was still grappling with an inner restlessness that kept me searching for more. Around this time, I was fortunate enough to be invited to a dinner event to learn more about cardiovascular medications. The experience created a strong visceral desire in me to work in the pharmaceutical industry: I was hooked! But the moment the spark was lit to work in Pharma, so too began the oscillation of the idea between my head and my heart, primarily because of the lukewarm support I received from family and friends. It is noteworthy that societal structures have a profound impact on humanity. They can affect our beliefs, our relationships, and who we ultimately choose to become.

While it is respectful to listen to the opinion of those around you, it is more important to listen to that loving whisper within and go where it leads you. You may need to muster up the courage to move forward with an unpopular idea because of potentially unsupportive and even antagonistic people. Some may hurl comments and exhibit behaviors that could really catch you off guard, and you may be the subject of gossip which can make you feel shunned and alone. For various reasons, some people don't like it when others want to reinvent themselves; this is a wall you may have to scale to move forward. But don't let those barriers stop you! No matter where you are in life or what you do, there will always be someone with your name in their mouth; such is life on the earth plane.

Anyway, I started the time-consuming task of modifying my resume and preparing for interviews. By 2004, I had booked a series of meetings with local recruiters. The first one I met with told me that some pharmaceutical companies liked to hire nurses, due to their knowledge of the human body and inherent collaboration with physicians. Who knew?!

Nurses are typically considered invaluable members of a patient's multidisciplinary team. Additionally, the recruiter recommended that I find someone in the Pharma industry to job shadow and see if I would like the work, given that it was such a departure from my nursing career.

So, I asked one of the doctors I worked with if he knew of any pharmaceutical reps, and he immediately provided a contact. I called this person and explained my situation, and he agreed to help. My request flowed rather seamlessly, as if an invisible force was assisting, which was indeed the case. And this is how Wilson became my mentor. Later, my Spirit Guides would tell me that an interconnection between *Spirit, Wilson, and me* had been orchestrated to wake me up, while leading me toward less depleting work in the corporate world. I felt a surge of excitement when I realized that my goal to work in pharmaceutical sales was within reach.

By June 2005, I had accomplished my career-change goal and eagerly left nursing behind to embrace a different reality as a territory manager, selling the cardiovascular medications that I had previously administered to patients. Despite my enthusiasm, I was still very frightened to walk forward into the unknown but embraced it anyway as I headed right into the company's comprehensive training program. It felt like I had a new lease on life, which quelled that restlessness for a while. The following year I would experience the synchronistic events with Wilson that I referenced in the beginning, and although these seemed to come out of the blue, I now understand that Spirit placed me in energetic lockstep with Wilson to alchemize those synchronicities onto the earth plane. This is similar to how an electric conductor or catalyst works. In time, the interconnection between *Spirit, Wilson, and me* faded, as seamlessly as it had formed. Its spiritual purpose had been served.

On April 17, 2006, and at the not-so-tender age of thirty-eight, something unexpected and life-changing happened! Early that morning, I jumped out of bed and headed to the local Tim Hortons restaurant for coffee, which was not out of the ordinary for me (yeah, I'm a caffeine junky). By this time, I had read a book called *Natural Born Intuition* by Lauren Thibodeau, Ph.D. I felt that her message gave me permission to continue observing the world in the way I had been doing for likely all of my life. This way of being in the world looks at the potential for everything we see, hear, and notice as indicators of something else at play in our lives. So, while driving up the street in darkness, I saw two rabbits hopping playfully along a neighboring front lawn; for me this symbolized a symbiotic relationship between two people. I was drawn to them and wondered if it was a sign of something to come.

An Unexpected Conversation

I arrived at Tim's, ordered two coffees, and then drove back home as the sky began to brighten. I parked the car and proceeded to walk toward the front door of the house and gasped as I looked down and saw what appeared to be a mangled animal on the walkway to the door! How had I not seen it earlier? What could it possibly mean? Well, before noon that day, I found out! I was sitting in the kitchen having a rather unplanned and profound conversation with my husband, when the words, "it's over" spilled out of my mouth; I was done with the marriage, that was it! Admittedly, I had contemplated the impact of a potential divorce on our family for a few years prior to that fateful day, but it just sat there in the back of my mind because of the concern I felt for my children. I had had no plans to end the marriage when I got out of bed that morning and thought, *did Spirit just take the wheel*?! Within a flash, I felt a sickening yet liberating feeling as I realized that I was going to have to create a new life for myself and my children, not chaperoned by a spouse, parents, family, or friends.

Although I fully embraced motherhood, I saw myself peeling away from other roles which put me in the center of a social storm. However, in my naiveté, I didn't realize that following that inner niggle would translate into the complete loss of my support system and in time, almost every member of the entire clan. I quickly found out who my friends were; I can tell you that few remained. Although these individuals were meant to fall away at some point to allow my soul to expand, it still hurt like hell and caused a lot of sadness in my everyday life. It was during this tumultuous time that I stumbled onto a book by Dr. Wayne Dyer called *The Power of Intention* and it quickly became my therapist during this dark period of my life. Later, I realized that in my case, divorce was a necessary part of my soul's growth, even though it felt like I was self-destructing at that time.

I imagine that I looked like a nomad to the outside world as I changed homes, jobs, and people. But each change was necessary for my life to be cracked wide open so I could become free to be the truest expression of myself. Shedding the old Paula shell, albeit painful, has made me feel more like a diamond than a piece of coal. However, when I reflect on those disruptive years, I wonder if my energetic self, that auric layer of potential around the body, literally endured what carbon goes through to become a diamond. My new path was filled with countless experiences of swimming against the societal current through a sea of constant change, with a few tsunamis thrown in, metaphorically speaking.

My dream of a life partnership might have been in tatters at that moment, but I still believed in the possibility of an enduring love; a truly wholesome partnership wherein we both could thrive. So, one afternoon that summer, having announced my need to leave my marriage and being in the midst of the emotional maelstrom of getting on with a new life, I found myself in a home décor store that I had never even heard of before. I came across a 30" x 38" framed print of the most romantic couple imaginable embracing in front of the Eiffel tower in Paris, France. I stared wondrously at it and quietly said to myself, "I want that kind of love someday." I was drawn in for some reason and purchased the print without hesitation. As the years passed, I would take that print everywhere I moved, ensuring that it took center stage in each home I occupied. I became familiar with the concept of vision boards and so I referred to it as such, as I dreamed about who my future husband was, what he might look like, and how we would live our life together.

By January 2007, I made a difficult decision to resign from my cherished pharmaceutical job as well; I suspect that Spirit was fine with it because its purpose—to make contact with me—had been served; however, I did not leave empty-handed. I threw those transferable skills over my shoulder and off I went to a number of other jobs, until I finally landed in the medical device industry, which is where I am to this day. Despite all this, I am so grateful to share that my precious children have grown up to become strong, healthy, and happy adults. Only now do I fully understand that a restless niggle is an important feeling to chisel through to rediscover, redefine, and reconstruct your most authentic self. My journey to this point had been long and tiresome, and it wasn't over yet!

Reflection:

Holy moly! I was constantly readjusting to my surroundings; no wonder I was so tired! People may not understand what your soul is calling you to do, but I encourage you to follow that niggle despite what others may say; for it may lead you directly to your life purpose (AKA your North Star), which is woven deep within and is meant for the highest good of all concerned. When you shine, the collective consciousness benefits. So, be prepared to roll up your sleeves and do the work it will take to find out who you truly are and what good you are meant to contribute to the world. And know that your contribution will have a reverberating effect across the Universe.

3

Manifester Moves

"We do not describe the world we see,
we see the world we can describe."

~ RENÉ DESCARTES (1596–1650)

If I'd known that my work toward a deeper, more fulfilling life had only just begun, I might not have stayed the course for all the years required to complete this next leg of the journey. The good news is that I had a visceral desire to keep going as I searched through the debris of my restlessness to find peace, stability, and perhaps self-love. Given all that I was grappling with, I turned to books for resolve and chose titles that could help me decode the aberrations swirling around me, while seeking a way to move toward a better life; in short, books became my best friends. At first, I was drawn to the self-help section at bookstores, and eventually, I embraced the new-age genre. I dove in, devouring every word of each book I purchased and resurfaced with at least one fresh pearl between my teeth. It's surprising that

I would take to books at all because I hadn't enjoyed reading in high school, not even a little bit; but I began to enjoy the process of finding and reading a good book, knowing that it could be a source of inspiration to heal me from the emotional motion sickness of constant change.

As an aside, I thought it would be of value to provide a list, albeit not exhaustive, of some of the books I have read along the way. I would like to say a heartfelt thank you to all the authors who have shared stories reflecting their personal perception and words of wisdom through their masterpieces. I hope that many of the following books will resonate with you, if you haven't indulged in them already:

- *The Alchemist* by Paolo Coelho
- *Angels in My Hair* by Lorna Byrne
- *Ask and It Is Given* by Esther and Jerry Hicks
- *Astrophysics for People in a Hurry* by Neil deGrasse Tyson
- *Becoming Supernatural* by Dr. Joe Dispenza
- *Care of the Soul* by Thomas Moore
- *The Celestine Prophecy* by James Redfield
- *Contacting Your Spirit Guide* by Sylvia Browne
- *Discovering the Medium Within* by Anysia Kiel

- *Dr. Judith Orloff's Guide to Intuitive Healing* by Dr. Judith Orloff
- *Easy Lenormand Handbook* by Marcus Katz and Tali Goodwin
- *The Future is Yours: Do Something About It!* by Raymon Grace
- *Glynis Has Your Number* by Glynis McCants
- *To Heaven and Back* by Mary C. Neal, M.D.
- *The Hidden Messages in Water* by Masaru Emoto
- I *See Your Dream Job* by Sue Fredrick
- *Man's Search for Meaning* by Viktor Frankl
- *Mind Waves* by Betty Shine
- *Nutrition for Intuition* by Doreen Virtue and Robert Reeves
- *Power of the Soul* by John Holland
- *The Power of Your Subconscious Mind* by Dr. Joseph Murphy
- *The Present* by Spencer Johnson
- *Proof of Heaven* by Eben Alexander, M.D.
- *The Purpose of Your Life* by Carol Adrienne
- *Remembering the Future* by Colette Baron-Read
- *Sacred Contracts* by Caroline Myss
- *The Secret* by Rhonda Byrne

- *Soul Stories* by Gary Zukav
- *The Spontaneous Healing of Belief* by Gregg Braden
- *Trust your Vibes* by Sonia Choquette
- *Your Guide to the Tarot* by Janet Berres

As I began to try new things, I fully embodied the saying: *throw spaghetti at the wall and see what sticks.* It required a lot of pasta with a few meatballs thrown in, but over time I learned that the secret sauce is action! It seemed that I was moving something in every area of my life, and those experiences, in turn, were moving me inward. For me, this did not lead to a routine practice of quiet meditation in a Zen garden. Spirit knew that I wasn't going to be very successful with that, so instead, I naturally adopted a sort of walking meditation through life, quietly observing the world around me. To this day, I am constantly straddling the line between the earthly and etheric realms; however, I have come to understand that they are one. I began to embrace each new adventure, whether it involved changing homes, exploring distinct roles in various organizations, or meeting new people. What was so powerful about these experiences was the unexpected byproduct of manifesting new opportunities into my life, a benefit of the *inward* part. As new opportunities rolled in,

I could see that my positive mindset was propelling my desires to fruition. Would you like to hear about a few experiences that I have manifested into my life, with Spirit's help of course?

In 2007, I tripped over manifesting while I was in the process of changing homes. I was renting a condo in Burlington, Ontario, when I decided that I wanted to buy my very first home as a single woman while my children were still young. It was a big, bold step for me, but one I felt compelled to take. I had signed a lease agreement for the condo which meant that I needed to find someone to take over the rent so that I could exit the agreement prematurely. I made the conscious decision to visualize what I hoped for and felt a playful excitement believing that I would be able to make this wish come true. Weeks later, there was a seemingly random knock at the door, and when I answered, I saw a woman I had never seen before. She told me that she saw a posting downstairs in the main lobby about the unit I was renting; but here's the bizarre part, neither the condo owner nor I had posted anything about the unit being available for rent. This mysterious woman liked the condo very much, but we never heard from her again. However, I didn't lose faith and had a feeling that this *fluke* had meaning, as if my desire was closer to becoming a reality; I felt a supercharged-quickening feeling as a result of her visit. Perhaps we should refer to this visit as a synchronicity; Cambridge Dictionary defines it as, *"… the happening by chance of two or more related or similar events at the same time"*.[8] Soon afterwards, a divorced father of two came by, and not only did he want to rent the condo, but he also asked to buy my children's bunk beds for his two children, who were around the same age as mine. Cool, eh?

A Bizarre Synchronicity

Here is another example of a bizarre synchronicity. I was interviewing for a job opportunity at what I will refer to as Company A, but I truly wanted a job that was available at Company B. As I was sitting in the front lobby of Company A, waiting to go in for the interview, I happened to look down and saw a blue recycling bin on the floor with a piece of paper stuck to the side that had the name of Company B on it! How could this be? Company B was likely twenty minutes away by car and there was no affiliation as far as I knew. Again, I felt a supercharged-quickening feeling at such a strange occurrence, it wasn't just a piece of paper with words on it, the experience carried a very exciting energy with it. So, I harnessed that energy of excitement by staying upbeat and applied for my desired job at Company B. Shortly thereafter, I received an invitation to interview, which kept the excitement flowing through, as I stayed positive and visualized myself being offered the position by the hiring manager; it paid off because I was hired for the position I preferred at Company B, yay! But wait, there's more! I settled into my position quite nicely, but then we began to hear some irrefutable objections about one of the company's anchor products.

About a year later, the associates in our division were let go one by one, and I was one of them! How could this be? How could I put so much good juju into something that turned out to be all wrong for me? Could that role have been some kind of booby prize? The pain of being jobless was real, but about six months later I found myself in a new role with a caring boss who led a hard-working team selling a solid product line. I did not intend to manifest a job loss, but greater forces were at work to break me down, which in the end, made me stronger. Life is filled with ups and downs which are aptly designed to teach us lessons to become the best we can be, not just for ourselves but for others as well.

Here is another job-related example of wishing and receiving through the process of manifestation—but this time, there was a happier outcome. I had been working in a medical device company for years and was starting to feel tremendous restlessness in my role. By this time, I was more consciously aware of my intentions and the subsequent synchronicities that materialized; I would also make comments to Spirit about their blatant chess moves. Around this time, as I was ruminating about my next move in the company, I was informed that two company directors were speaking about me and wondering if I would be interested in making a move into a different function within the organization; and with that my desire was lit!

Well, didn't I run into trouble with my computer? I was frustrated that it couldn't be fixed remotely, so I packed it up in preparation to take it upstairs for the IT associate to diagnose the issue. While on the way, I had a sudden inkling to take a detour to check out our newly renovated cafeteria, and who was sitting there alone in the room? It was the hiring manager for this new role I'd been considering. I thought to myself, *well, that's convenient* and thanked Spirit for help with this connection. I walked over, said hello, and began chatting. Would you believe that I kept bumping into her after that—in the washroom, in the halls, and so forth. I felt excited knowing that Spirit was seemingly working behind the scenes. Finally, after a lengthy process, I was hired for the role! The same kind of thing happened some years later when I wanted to move into a new role within the organization. Synchronicities played out and I got that job as well. I couldn't have been more grateful.

From a non-scientific perspective and my personal point of view, I believe that once we become awakened to a desire, we tap into unseen forces which can help us turn that desire into a reality; and many things can happen along the way to achieving it. The magic happens during the span of time leading up to and including the achieved desire; that is when a blend of earthly and ethereal forces work together to achieve your goal. But remember, those ethereal forces can push their own agenda—as we saw with "my" desire to work at Company B—in order for incremental growth to occur. And yes, there are light and shadowy forces that can pull our strings at times; however, I *choose* to focus my energy toward the light. Those loving and all-knowing ethereal forces were instrumental in moving me through many changes over the years and, as a result, my vibrational frequency got a boost which enabled me to communicate telepathically with Spirit.

Let's dissect manifesting from a high level using the example of a desire to purchase a home. It takes a conscious awareness to strike a desire, and it is imperative to note that Spirit is often the force igniting your awareness to it. Perhaps the impetus to purchasing a home is because you won the lottery, or you need to move because of a job change, or your family is increasing in size, or there is a squabble between you and a neighbor, etc. The list of impetuses is endless. Once we become aware of something we desire, the chatter begins within the recesses of our mind and heart, and that is when an intention is born. We start to engage our imagination and visualize the home we would like to live in as excitement creeps in. We take practical steps like searching for houses online, or driving around a community to get ideas, or contacting a realtor, or meeting with a financial advisor, and so on.

An Invitation for Spirit

While we go about this process, we may also be praying for assistance; note that asking is an invitation for Spirit to get involved to help your desire become a reality. As you well know, the process of searching for a home can be quite stressful, which may keep you leaning into your faith through prayer. At some point, while on the hunt for a place to live, you may encounter unseen forces through signs, symbols, and synchronicities—thanks to Spirit—which ratchet up your excitement and propel you forward; that super-charged-quickening feeling in the heart center raises your vibration. If the stars align—keeping in mind that we all have some degree of free will—then the pieces of the puzzle fall into place, which, in our example, leads to a physical move into your desired new home. The thought in your mind moves a feeling in your heart, which engages your faith and moves you forward toward your desire. This is a rather simplified explanation of the mind-body-spirit connection, but I think you get my drift. Imagine what happens when we layer in the physical, emotional, mental, and spiritual aspects of a human being, and then plug that person into Source energy; seeing that individual's truest potential would be staggering and incomprehensible.

Earlier, I mentioned that the secret sauce to getting things to stick is action! When we take action, no matter how small, we engage ourselves and unseen forces in the creative process which alchemizes our new reality. But, when you call upon a higher power for assistance, you may get more than you bargained for (more life lessons). I would like to spend some time on the concept of action because fear-based thinking can keep us from taking it. Baby steps are a wonderful way to manifest a desire that you want to achieve; if you don't know which direction to go in then try this exercise. Imagine yourself as a mouse in a maze. If the path is clear, then lean into it and ask yourself, *do I feel good or bad*? Move toward that which feels good and continue to *feel* your way through the rest of the maze until you achieve your goal or reach an unplanned destination. If the path is blocked and you still feel pulled toward it, then lean into it and, again, ask yourself, *do I feel good or bad*? If you feel good, then find a way to move through the barrier. Go by feel and keep in mind that you are never alone, Source is always watching.

When I am providing intuitive guidance, I often hear myself urge others to move something in their lives. Move a thought from negative self-talk to a can-do attitude; or a feeling from jealousy to joy; or a cell from sluggish to sparkling; or limbs from idle to energized! Given the fear-based thinking we experienced globally during the pandemic, I felt *moved* to *manifest* something on social media to help others through this extremely difficult time. This was atypical for me, so I asked my grown children for help. And in keeping with the theme of this chapter on manifestation, I am sharing the details of my March Forward Series that was launched in March 2022, to help others move past COVID-19 and get busy manifesting their desires instead. Here we go:

The Purpose: To help you MOVE forward from your pandemic woes. May you feel bathed in a higher vibration and gush with gratitude and love.

The Process: Share a daily message from Spirit and highlight inspirational content to help you strengthen your physical, emotional, mental, and spiritual muscles.

The Payoff: Re-emerge from the pandemic feeling completely recharged and fully ALIVE!

I channeled thirty-one messages for this series— one for each day of the month—and they were intended for people who resonated with them whenever they came upon them. Please know that these channeled messages were not intended to match the daily topic; instead, they reflected my daily commitment to channel for whomever needed/needs a message from Spirit. Note that Spirit often speaks metaphorically. I would like to share those messages here; however, I modified some of the titles slightly and removed the inspirational content that I found on the internet to respect copyright laws. You will be able to find a plethora of information on the internet which best suit your needs. Perhaps one of these channeled messages will resonate with you as well, directly, or as a jump-off point to a new thought or idea. Come on! Let's strengthen those physical, emotional, mental, and spiritual muscles. And away we go!

March Forward Series

March 1, 2022:
Move those cells!

Channeled Message: This is the land of the Mississaugas, take note, the indigenous people who have gone before you are here. The children who hid in the caves bask in the glory of Source light rejoice— there are no stragglers, all have been accounted for and all are loved. For Mr. Sandman, the time has come for your dream to unfold, so sit up straight and get prepared for goodness, be goodness.

March 2, 2022:
I am grateful for every place my feet take me!

Channeled Message: Tell Matilda to let the dog out, his soul is shrinking indoors, free him from stagnancy, it's time to wake again. A German shepherd in your block needs extra attention, he is nearing the end of his life and needs a teaspoonful of love.

March 3, 2022:
Meditate in the bathroom!

Channeled Message: The future bishop will be non-binary which represents a growth and expansion that we have been waiting for. We express Source and Source expresses all. Congratulate him with an open heart and mind for you will be touched by the Angels for doing so.

March 4, 2022:
Eat more colorful foods!

Channeled Message: Jonathan needs a new bicycle, he has prayed and prayed for a big shiny red one, please make his wish come true, your reward is his great big smile. An aunt in spirit has stepped forward to try and save your keister, you can tell that it's her by all the yellow flowers you see everywhere, open your eyes to her love and assistance—your subconscious knows you need to make this change.

March 5, 2022:
Declutter to release stuck energy!

Channeled Message: Seeing a checkered flag, your trauma is finished, dead, done, over with. So, jump up and dust yourself off with a little attitude and loads of forgiveness—it's all done, the trauma bond has been broken and you can breathe fully again, and yes, money is coming in the form of a new job, if you take it, you will be different, you will be brand new.

March 6, 2022:
What do you focus on?

Channeled Message: Your bowels are bunged up; can't you see that your lungs are too? A foul release is needed, and bowel aids may be required, a spoonful of ground flax seeds will do wonders for you, so get going! Literally!

March 7, 2022:
Orgasms can help you heal!

Channeled Message: There is an aunt here in spirit, at three degrees of separation, and she is asking you to hold on tight, try one more time; third time's a charm and you will be able to patch things up with your hubby.

March 8, 2022:
Indulge your senses at a bakery!

Channeled Message: Throw a magic stone in the air, that's right, grab your favorite crystal and throw it up to us; we will magnetize it from beyond the veil;

it will become your good luck charm; money will
flow in.

March 9, 2022:

You can manifest money!

Channeled Message: There is an ending at the Vati-
can, it will turn heads and good will come from it.
You have to know that there are some very good
people emitting pure love to our Ukraine brothers
and sisters; join in! You won't be disappointed.

March 10, 2022:

Feel great with clip-in hair extensions!

Channeled Message: Marybeth has a brother in spirit
who would love to say hello! He loved the Indy
drag car races; still does from the other side. He
sends his love.

March 11, 2022:

Become aware of your ego's flaws to be happy!

Channeled Message: It has come to our attention that
you are not taking good care of yourself, caring
must start with the self, awareness must start with
the self; turn inward and listen to what your body is
asking of you. You must shine your own light; that
is what I intended when I agreed to send you to
Earth in human form; be light and be love.

March 12, 2022:

Watch the words you say to yourself and others for they are powerful!

Channeled Message: Exhale love, hope, peace, and healing in the form of blue skies to the planet and to those who are suffering; your life force is a force to be reckoned with.

March 13, 2022:

Check out numerology!

Channeled Message: Notice that everything is energy, take the time to quietly acknowledge this today; you may be able to see us trying to reach you!

March 14, 2022:

Choose clothes that boost your energy!

Channeled Message: Why do you go at a breakneck speed? Slow down, breathe deeply, and pace yourself; you'll get where you want to go a whole lot quicker and easier; it may even be more joyful too.
— Signed, Nirvana

March 15, 2022:

It's all about love, baby!

Channeled Message: He is going to have a wee little accident that will help him refocus; it won't be noticeable in the physical, but it will cause an incredibly positive shift from within for him. No fear, just Love.

March 16, 2022:

Love breeds love breeds love breeds love…

Channeled Message: The next glass of water you drink today will be infused with our healing vibration; quietly thank it before you ingest; mindfulness is as critical as water!

March 17, 2022:

Mei-lan's voice is heavenly!

Channeled Message: The number order is important. 1, 2, 3, 4, find a way to close the door. 5, 6, 7, 8, there is no need to negotiate. Step into your self-worth suit, the time is now!

March 18, 2022:

Light and dark exist behind closed doors, choose light!

Channeled Message: Oh, the aliens, they are coming, but have no fear, they've always been here. Everything is part of Prime Source Energy.

March 19, 2022:

Everything is alive, respect all things!

Channeled Message: It is important to love all. Loving people who have done you wrong is important for ascension.

March 20, 2022:

Eat some basil pesto!

Channeled Message: The kingpin will rise again but not without swimmer's ear. Plug those holes quickly to avoid the pain.

March 21, 2022:

The world is a reflection of our mind!

Channeled Message: Check out the Marx brothers. When was the last time you laughed hard? It can soften a Covid blow.

March 22, 2022:

Live your truth!

Channeled Message: The door is locking behind you; blow it a kiss and give love to all you must say goodbye to; it is time to move forward.

March 23, 2022:
Like the sound of LOVE!

Channeled Message: Find comfort in knowing that Source is fully aware of the mess we have playing out on the earthly plane; some people play better than others. Breathe in pure love and exhale peace to every nook and cranny on our planet.

March 24, 2022:
There is more than meets the eye!

Channeled Message: Roses are red, violets are blue Sugar and spice are coming to you; get excited!

March 25, 2022:
Traumatized brains can hurt!

Channeled Message: Get working on the project that is meant for you. Don't worry about what others think, nobody really cares anyway, they are busy in their own heads.

March 26, 2022:
Do some anti-aging for your brain!

Channeled Message: Tell Tabitha to get her groove on; don't make the same mistake twice.

March 27, 2022:

A channeler can enlighten!

Channeled Message: Just because you're blocked
doesn't mean you must abort your mission; find
another way to achieve your career goals. If you
are open to our help then, yes, we will help.

March 28, 2022:

Oneness can lead to happiness and love!

Channeled Message: Tip your thoughts, feelings,
and actions to the light side; the world benefits
when you shine your light!

March 29, 2022:

Heal...

Channeled Message: Cosmic showers are upon you;
don't be surprised nor fearful; just enjoy the
inner view.

March 30, 2022:

Extraterrestrials can do good things!

Channeled Message: Tell them that tit for tat is not
the way to go; move away from the heat of the
argument and send them love.

March 31, 2022:
Send global peace!

Channeled Message: Live, love, laugh it off; life is tough, and so is the gruff.

Reflection:

How would you describe your world? Do your thoughts, feelings, and behaviors reflect old programming that negatively impacts your view of it? Are you a "glass half empty" kind of person? What does your self-talk sound like? What kind of content do you spend time sifting through on television, social media, magazines, and so forth? Is it uplifting or light dimming? Have you read any good books lately? What is your body telling you? Do you listen? What are you feeling pulled to do? What do you need physically, emotionally, mentally, and spiritually to fill your cup? What actions do you need to take to feel fulfilled? What New Year's resolutions do you keep postponing? And why? What baby steps could you take to move toward your goals? Give yourself permission to accomplish your goals in various ways and get excited when you visualize yourself achieving them!

My experiences by this time, with the process of manifesting, truly enhanced my trust in Spirit and fostered confidence in myself. Admittedly, I've not been fully present on social media, and my self-talk reflected the fears I felt to put myself out there. But my desire to quell the collective fear from the pandemic, an event that I refer to as "scheduled" for our evolution, moved me into action; and with that the March Forward Series was launched. By intending to help others, I helped myself conquer my shyness on social media.

4

Otherworldly Encounters

"The supernatural is the natural not yet understood."
~ ELBERT HUBBARD (1856–1915)

I was sitting at the dining room table around 5:30 one morning playing with a tarot card deck when out of nowhere I saw a fruit fly buzzing around me. Naturally, I ignored it. But this guy was persistent and returned, so I did what most people do and immediately shooed it away. Insistent that I respond, he came flying past my face again, so I yelled, "what do you want?" The next thing that happened still amazes me to this day, as I immediately fell into a trance-like state where my arms and legs kept moving, but my mind seemed to have been shelved for some reason. Moments later, I observed myself getting up from the chair and proceeded to walk downstairs to the bathroom mirror. There, I turned around to look at my back and, to my horror, was a big black spider crawling on the shoulder of my pink housecoat! OMG! The trance evaporated instantly, and that spider nearly lost its life as I dropped my housecoat to the floor. I came away from this bizarre experience feeling grateful for the chance to observe myself and watch as Spirit protected me, through a sweet little fruit fly. That was an inexplicably powerful demonstration of how visible and non-visible forces work together to help us; I was literally between two worlds in that moment; which is really actually one.

I remember sharing my fruit fly experience with a gentleman in our family and I could feel his brain screaming, "this lady's crazy!" While I find it funny, I completely understand. You could chalk any synchronous event you've ever had up to coincidence, and some people do. But put them all together and you have to start thinking, "Hey, wait a minute. Stop the train! There's something going on here!" In fact, here's an idea: why not start keeping a journal of all the synchronous experiences that happen to you? And for goodness' sake, don't judge them or yourself. Judgement stunts our growth, and the lack of appreciation for all things created by Source blocks us from living an extraordinary life. You block You! Listen, I know how difficult it is to release the mind from judgement, I wrestle with it too. But I have come to see that this is one of the most liberating things we can do, and it's free!

As time went on, I continued to experience events that were stranger than fiction, and looking back, I can see that I was being taught that different realities and dimensions are a real thing. Not all my experiences have been as refreshing as being rescued from a giant spider. One incident, in particular, practically scared me to death! I awoke around 2:00 a.m. after having had a horrible dream where I felt like I was being sexually attacked by an invisible force that was ripe with male energy. I struggled to get free from this negative force and made so much noise that I woke my then-common-law partner, Imants (AKA Mancy, as Mom likes to call him). I didn't tell him about my horrible dream, or at least that's what I thought it was. Imants got up and made his way to the bathroom. Upon his return, he blurted out, "I just saw an orb!" An orb is a small circle of fast-moving spiritual energy. He said it zipped straight past his night table. Instantly I realized that my "horrible dream" was undoubtedly a psychic attack—in other words, there *was* something in the room, it hadn't been just a nightmare...a negative entity had snuck into my consciousness and jumped me!

I didn't understand the reason for the experience at the time, but later I understood that I was becoming more open to the non-visible spiritual realm; and with that, I knew that I needed to be more proactive and protect myself from negative forces. I knew the instant the orb exited because I felt myself suddenly relax. After I got over my panic, I proceeded to tell Imants about the horrible experience I had just had. We were both completely blown away by it. Note that orbs are not always laced with bad energy. I see orbs often as they move swiftly past with a loving and soothing energy; you know the difference by how you feel.

A few months later, I awoke around 2:30 a.m. to see a fast-moving group of white horizontal lines zipping back and forth in front of my face. I freaked and ducked my head under the covers! What the heck was that?! I saw this energy again on another night, but at least it was kind enough to remain in the corner of the room. People have suggested this kind of thing is due to an "overactive imagination," or being in a dreamy sleep state. But these experiences were super real to me: they were exceedingly bizarre and unexpected, they had no obvious cause, and they felt terribly ominous. And they scared the boots off me!

Not all experiences were completely without cause, however. On the topic of "don't try this at home," I had the urge to communicate telepathically one night with Imants' sister, who had died at the age of twelve when a young female driver jumped the curb at a crosswalk, striking and killing her instantly; although I wasn't doing energy channeling back then (ha-ha we all do it), I was drawn to experiment with it. The next morning, my daughter reported that she had felt like she was floating above her mattress during the night; and knowing what I was up to telepathically, I was freaked right out!

Although I had thought that Imants just might be The One for me, after about four years, our romantic relationship had fizzled, so we agreed to be friends, which led to his departure. But our connection grew into a platonic love which felt more alive, peaceful, and purer than ever before; it was a "brother from another mother" kind of feeling. So, although we were not going to "go the distance" romantically, there had been a purpose to our relationship. Intuitively, I could see that we had a soul contract to stabilize each other and develop new skills. Imants morphed into a brilliant home renovator which had been evident by the work he had done in our home; and now it's his greatest passion, talent, and contribution to the world. Additionally, he had endured a great deal of heartbreak over the years, having suffered the loss of several loved ones in his family; and my new ability to channel permitted me to connect spiritually with his grandmother, stepmother, father, and of course, his little stepsister. This was organic for me and healing for him. How, you ask? In time, Imants began to understand that his family members were not gone at all, but rather, they existed in an energetic form; in essence, Imants was the first person for whom I actively channeled in my personal life, my first "client" if you will. In 2023, Spirit told me that Imants and I had been "brothers in arms" (fellow soldiers) in a past life. This made sense given that Imants was a part of the Canadian armed forces in this lifetime and is fiercely overprotective of everyone he cares for. In short, he is an Earth angel and one that I will cherish forever. He jokingly calls himself Mancy-guru, to which we lovingly roll our eyes and chuckle. We love you, Mancy.

The Man at the Desk

Another otherworldly event occurred in our home while I was with Imants when my daughter witnessed a man in spirit sitting at our desk in the office; she said that it looked like he was doing paperwork. I also had a strange apparitional experience one afternoon in that same house while standing in my son's room talking with my children. I looked over to the door at one point and saw a headless ghost sprinting down the hallway toward my daughter's bedroom, holy crap!

It's easy to dismiss one strange experience as an anomaly—a trick of the imagination, or the result of too much stress or too little sleep. But when the bizarre experiences start piling up, you have to take them seriously. You have to figure there's something going on that defies everything anyone has ever taught you about what is "real." I know I sure did. It's kind of like those "connect the dots" puzzles we did as children. You draw a line from one "dot" to the next one. Then another dot shows up. You connect to it. And another dot shows up. Before long you're staring at a half-finished drawing of something, and you're not yet sure what it is. But you keep connecting the dots. It is engaging and intriguing. What is it that's being revealed?! I was hooked! In time, I would come to appreciate each transmission from Spirit as a sacred breadcrumb from the etheric realm; they range from simple to darn right wild, and I ate 'em all up! The act of connecting the dots is like watching a bouncing ball move from word to word in a sing-along-type sentence; except that when observing spiritual messages, the *word* may be a sign, a symbol, a synchronicity, or some other communication that comes your way at any given time; oh, and by the way, I am not special, we all can develop our own energetic language with Spirit. Although I was not born into an indigenous culture in this lifetime, I feel that my connection with Spirit follows a more aboriginal pattern than a strictly "religious" one.

I marvel at Spirit's tenacity because when they want to magnetize you toward a connection for your soul's evolution, they make it happen whether you're aware of it, and agree to it, or not; your free will gets tossed out the window. This was the case when Spirit synchronized an encounter between a former colleague and me, whom I hadn't seen in over a decade; I will refer to him as Peter. I had no idea why Spirit would reacquaint us after so much time had passed as I had no need, nor desire, to speak with him, but leave it to Spirit to create the reason. So, early on the morning of January 14, 2016, at the age of forty-eight, I was sitting at the dining room table when all of a sudden, I felt as though an elephant was sitting on my chest, and I knew exactly what that meant. I went to the hospital and had the usual cardiac workup done, which I was very familiar with, having previously been an ER Nurse. I fully expected to have two sets of cardiac enzymes drawn, along with an electrocardiogram (ECG)—which measures the electrical activity of the heart. Given that I had no previous cardiac issues, the attending ER physician would ask me to follow up with my family doctor once the results were back, which typically took about eight hours.

Well, that is not what happened! All of a sudden, I began to feel my heart beat faster than I had ever experienced before. I wondered, was it SVT (supraventricular tachycardia), which is an abnormally fast heart rhythm. Sheer panic came over me, as my nurse brain jumped through an array of possible causes. Then, I saw the young ER doctor look over at me with worry in his eyes, which freaked me out even more. He ordered the nurse to give me sedation under the tongue, then hung a liter of intravenous fluid, and did a stat ECG. I looked up toward the nursing station after the ECG was done and saw two people studying my results; I asked the doctor how it looked, given that I knew how to interpret rhythms; he said the nurses were trying to figure it out because it looked unusual. All I thought was, *what the heck is going on with me*? Shortly after that, the ER physician told me that I couldn't go home because of the electrical event, and that I'd need a consult with the on-call Specialist. Well, guess who walked in a few hours later; it was Peter. He ordered a Holter monitor (portable ECG machine) and a stress test;

and when I asked about the unusual rhythm, he said that it was fine; my test results came back normal, so I was discharged from his care.

Naturally, the whole heart thing kept me feeling puzzled for quite some time. Why did my heart display such stress only to find out that all was normal? What was the point, and why did Spirit bring Peter back from the past (put a pin in it)?! Instantly, I knew that something was up because the feeling of those puppeteer strings held by Spirit (synchronicity) were more formidable and palpable than ever before. I knew the very moment we intersected that Peter would be important for my journey, and indeed he was.

That year I sought a reading from someone who predicts the future by way of Turkish coffee grounds—they arrange themselves at the bottom of a coffee cup after you drink the beverage; and the reader looks at the shapes, patterns, and so much more to provide you with information. This man said many things that resonated, but one of the last things he shared was, "you're going to marry a man from out of the country; this man has one son." Although I knew never to give my power away to a reader (by believing what they say is the absolute truth), and I understood that messages received may or may not be meant for me directly, I still believed that some of the information provided might be helpful; having said that, I couldn't get this reader's message out of my head. Who in the world could this man be?

An Unshakeable Urge

Shortly after my electrical event, I had the unshakeable urge to contact Peter, and it appeared to happen rather seamlessly. Once we connected, I noticed that our banter over text carried on as if we'd known each other our whole lives, which was not at all the case, but there was a strange familiarity with him that I had never known before. In time, it began to feel like Spirit had cast a spell that kept us magnetized to one another over the next few years, all through a series of signs, symbols, and synchronicities. Our hearts felt padlocked, and Spirit held the key.

Over time, our reacquaintance would turn into friendship, which morphed into fondness and, eventually, love; even though he was not free to love me in a way that I truly deserved. Our relationship had supernatural overtones and it resembled the notion of a twin flame connection (twin flames share the same soul), although, I am not entirely sold on that. However, the unfoldment of these strange events between *Spirit, Peter, and me* would ultimately bookend the beginning phase of the supernatural chapter of my life highlighted, as it was, by energetic interconnections (trio bonds) with others (and fruit flies too), all of which had been marked by an initiation that involved *Spirit, Wilson, and me.*

Allow me to provide more context about what I refer to as a trio bond. We are all connected beings with the potential of becoming interconnected (entangled). However, I chose to identify those three-way interconnections as trio bonds, because of the synchronous events that were puppeteered by Spirit for the expansion of my supernatural awareness. Each was imperative for my own understanding to write *Fruit Fly Intelligence* for you.

Over the next five years or so, I wasn't able to see the purpose of the trio bond between *Spirit, Peter, and me* because I was expected to move through it on a day-to-day basis in order to experience tailored signs, symbols, and synchronicities involving Peter. Spirit did what they always do, which is place one bread crumb on my path at a time, when I wished I could have had the whole loaf! Would we bother to get into relationships if we knew they came with an expiration date? I know I wouldn't, but predestined interconnections are laced with soul lessons that we are supposed to experience in one lifetime or another, point-blank period. You know just as well as I do that we have to move through them to get to the pot of gold at the end of the rainbow, or the lump of coal, or piece of shit, keeping it real! Actually, every connection holds invaluable life lessons and character-building opportunities that are meant to help us achieve self-love, and our radiant self-love lights up the Universe. You matter! Throughout the remainder of *Fruit Fly Intelligence*, I will share a few of the mysterious things that happened with Peter's re-emergence into my life, and what I experienced as we were lockstepped with Spirit.

This newly formed trio bond between *Spirit, Peter, and me* left me with many questions, and given that I am innately curious, I leaned into divination tools (AKA fortune telling) and psychic readers to find some answers about the strange situation in which I found myself. I contacted a local psychic I had seen a few times before. This fascinating woman pulled out the usual tools from her psychic toolbelt to unpack the great mysteries of my life, only this time, she did something a bit different that was quite surprising: she pulled out a thirty-six-card deck called "Lenormand" which I'd never seen before, along with a homemade chart on which she placed the cards. She revealed many things that day, but of particular interest was regarding Peter, who was apparently very intrigued by my intuition; and she saw a potential romance with us over the next couple of years.

I wasn't accustomed to using any psychic tools given that I would never have considered myself skilled in this way; it's a world that felt completely foreign to me, but for some strange reason, I became fixated on learning about the history of the Lenormand deck, and how one could extract information from it. I went to the local bookstore to purchase a basic version for myself and settled on the *Fairy Lenormand Oracle Cards* by Marcus Katz, Tali Goodwin, and Davide Corsi. I read the little how-to book that came in the box and learned that the Lenormand deck was originally used centuries ago as a parlor game (AKA The Game of Hope).[9] As a newbie, I also decided to spend time watching videos to gain a better understanding about this kind of clairvoyance (future predictions), which is also referred to as cartomancy when using playing cards.[10] I was drawn in thanks to Spirit, you're so clever!

Shortly thereafter, I purchased a second deck by Marcus Katz and Tali Goodwin called the *Easy Lenormand Handbook*. There are many versions available today which have been embraced by countless mystics both on and off social media platforms around the world. The deck had been renamed after a famous nineteenth-century French fortune-teller, Miss Marie Anne Adelaide Lenormand. (1772–1843).[11]

One day, I awoke and decided to start the day by shuffling and then picking three cards from the deck with the intention of seeing what the morning, afternoon, and evening would bring. Once I became a little more comfortable with the practice, I embraced a daily morning routine of expanding my interaction with the cards by experimenting with different spreads. I was hooked and couldn't get enough! A few months later, I remembered that I had purchased a tarot deck the previous year, but once I had brought it home and unboxed it, I had grown uncomfortable with some of the less warm and fuzzy images, like the tower, the devil, and other shadowy cards. I accepted that I wasn't ready to use Tarot, but soon after becoming acquainted with the Lenormand decks, I took it out of my dresser drawer and dove right in.

These divination tools provide a visual representation of the supernatural realm. I developed a respect and understanding for the information and foresight they provided. If you would like to purchase a deck for yourself, then I recommend purchasing one that you feel drawn to, especially the one that your physical body leans into. Hold them, shuffle them, and speak to them with loving intentions and ask clear questions; notice colors, shapes, patterns, numbers, timing, and your feeling with each draw to garner valuable information for the answers you seek. As a channeler, I have come to appreciate that the environment around us is one giant tarot card; and a deck is a wonderful way to learn that.

Reflection:

Alas, the fruit fly enters the scene! This particular event was the most influential experience, which made me aware that Spirit can channel through everything! I came to understand that the Universe is fully alive and conscious! During this time, I was drinking through the proverbial firehouse of spiritual lessons. Sometimes I wonder how I stayed so sane through the steady stream of otherworldly encounters; and the heart-gripping entanglement that had only just begun between *Sprit, Peter, and me.* My encounter with that sweet little fruit fly became a refreshing reminder that I was not alone, and that I was actually being protected; and loved by my Spirit Guides. Because of all this and so much more, the supernatural is natural to me. I am sure you've had some unusual experiences of your own; I encourage you to write them down so that you can revisit them and garner important information that is meaning-ful to you.

5

Five Hearts and an Angel

*"When angels visit us, we do not hear the rustle of
wings, nor feel the feathery touch of the breast
of a dove; but we know the presence by
the love they create in our hearts."*

~ MARY BAKER EDDY (1821–1910)

I looked down at my left arm where two bruises
had appeared, likely from the boxes I carried that
week. They didn't really register until I took a closer look, when the bruises were turning yellow and
starting to fade. I could see two marks in the shape
of a heart, so, on May 12, 2016, I quickly snapped
a photo as I grappled with disbelief! The bruise fur-
thest from my elbow, away from my mole, was certainly more obvious than the other one below. I was
absolutely flabbergasted!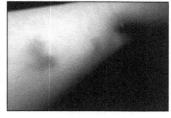
One of my friends saw
the image and jokingly
said, "it looks like the
stigmata or something."

I honestly didn't know what to make of it at first, but given the steady stream of signs, symbols, and synchronicities that I'd already experienced, along with bizarre events like: telepathy on steroids, a face shapeshifting, a headless ghost runner, an uninvited psychic attacker, a meetup with a protective fruit fly, why *not* two bruises in the shape of a heart as well?! With the expansion of my intuitive awareness, I finally understood that it was my Spirit Guides coming through loud and clear; as you can see they can be rather cheeky! With these photographs as evidence, I became more open to their love. Later, I understood that these images would be used to tell my story; and we all know that a picture is worth a thousand words.

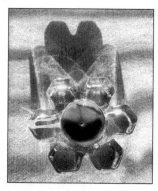

On February 16, 2017, I would experience the most salient and astounding experience of my entire life, outside of giving birth to my two beautiful babies. In fact, this supernatural encounter was the tipping point to my understanding that communication with Spirit is bidirectional. It was mid-afternoon and I was home alone sitting at the dining room table when I suddenly heard a young, peppy, female voice shout, "Can you see it? Can you see it?" Being the only person in the house, I was utterly gobsmacked! It seemed like the voice was coming from my right side, and out of thin air! But when I looked down, I noticed a heart-shaped silhouette above the snowflake candle holder that I had placed on the table for the holidays. In that moment, it dawned on me that I'd heard her voice before. She had woken me up in the middle of the night by whispering "Paula!" I was so excited to be able to hear her voice as clear as day, and in the afternoon no less! Check out the lovely image that this voice wanted me to notice.

This was *the* pivotal moment in my life when I became certain that communication with Spirit is a two-way street and not a figment of my imagination. I also realized that I was meant to connect with the spirit realm to help others in this lifetime. But at the time, I wasn't entirely sure what that would look like. I became aware that my physical, emotional, mental, and spiritual bodies were being metamorphosized into one so that I could see, hear, smell, taste, feel and sense the energetic language of the Universe. And truly speak with Spirit!

However, that miraculous moment when I heard Spirit speak turned into an immediate sadness as I remembered a female patient I'd met in the early 1990s, when I was a student nurse. I had been assigned to complete a mental health rotation, shadowing another nurse on the unit. One day this nurse informed me that I would be joining her for an outreach home visit. So, we drove to the home of a schizophrenic patient to see how she was doing with her family. I think it struck a nerve within because this young, vibrant, attractive-looking woman was around the same age as me and, sadly, we found her wandering around her home in a complete state of confusion. It was heartbreaking to watch, and ultimately became one of those moments that I will never forget as long as I live.

But, as I sat in front of this heart on my dining room table in 2017, far more intuitively tuned in than I was back then, I wondered what this meant for others who claimed to hear voices too, just as the schizophrenic patient did? I mean, seriously?! For me, this discovery was jaw-dropping! I personally had suffered from OCD as a child, twirled on the spot for most of my tweens, had been filled with anxiety for most of my life, and now I could hear voices too! Perhaps my life would have had a different outcome if I'd been diagnosed with a mental illness and prescribed medications to "normalize" me.

Please know that I realize the gravity of my words and fully comprehend the sensitivity of this topic. Since I am not a doctor, I cannot speak about anyone's mental journey other than my own. However, I wonder if the young woman I visited as a student nurse almost three decades ago had heard voices in the same way that I do now. My intuitive abilities bestowed by Spirit have enabled me to deliver future predictions, provide messages from loved ones who have crossed over, diminish people's pain by hovering with my hands, and provide intuitive guidance; and I am so incredibly humbled and honored to be able to do this work for others. What's more, I am a stable and solid member of society, hold down a great job, run a small business, and I've co-parented my beautiful children into healthy, happy, productive adults.

"Go Faster! Go Faster!"

Months after I'd heard that young, peppy, female voice at the dining room table, she came through again, only this time, I was driving hurriedly in my car with the expectation of being late for a customer meeting. I'm accustomed to driving within the speed limit, much to the chagrin of my grown children, but in this instance, I heard the voice shout "Go faster! Go faster!" so I trusted the message, pressed on the gas (sorry officers), and sailed quickly along the highway without any issue at all and, yes, I made it in perfect time for the meeting.

Sometime in 2017, I decided to meet up with my friend Donna, a medium and tarot card reader. During our session, she informed me that this young, peppy, female voice is one of my Spirit Guides and her name is Rosepetal. She went on to say that Rosepetal is a young indigenous girl who walks with a cat. What fascinates me about this revelation is how much it reminds me of the beautiful Precious Moments figurine and the Sandicast cat who have been with me since the days of my skating performances in Japan. I had been drawn to them for some reason—perhaps the sweet little Precious Moments figurine and the Sandicast cat represented Rosepetal and the cat who walks alongside her. I love all animals, but I have always gravitated toward cats; and now, I have a fondness for fruit flies too. I am sharing this because I am now able to see that these two ornaments, which I was drawn to so long ago, are an actual representation of two of the Guides (spiritual gatekeepers) who surround me with added protection when I am channeling. I have taken to the name Rosepetal as the Spirit who came through on that cold afternoon with a young, peppy, female voice; and I imagine a cat by her side.

It's truly astounding how we can be drawn to inanimate objects and not consciously understand why, but somewhere deep within our subconscious mind, we have an awareness of their significance. So, if you are keen to learn more about your life purpose, your environment, or simply want to understand more about yourself and those around you, then I recommend this exercise. Take a silent, open-minded, non-judgmental, multi-sensory walk about your home. See everything that surrounds you, notice what you are drawn to, and try listening for telepathic messages; just let those thoughts flow in without censorship, and then write them down. Notice subtle details; for example, it wasn't until I began writing about my Precious Moments figurine in this book that I noticed her headband was filled with hearts, and here I am sharing images of hearts that were sent to me by Spirit! Everything is energy; therefore, seemingly insignificant things may be filled with copious amounts of information for you to explore.

I saw another heart on April 7, 2017. This image appeared in the middle of my kitchen floor, and no, I didn't set this one up either! Now, I can imagine that

you're probably thinking, *that's a shabby looking heart, Paula*! But we're not talking about using our logical mind here, we're talking about using our instant intuition; it's a whole different ball game.

From my intuitive experiences to date, I have come to appreciate the nuances with every sign, symbol, and synchronicity, but I don't automatically launch into a game of twenty questions when they appear; in fact, it doesn't take work for me at all to draw any conclusions from them. If they resonate, then I will begin the process of analyzing them, and typically, I go with my first impression. With that in mind, the image looks like a heart to me. Perhaps to someone else it could look like a bird, which would likely have meaning for that individual. The key here is that you go with *your* first impression, which is the best way to process those tailored messages that Spirit is sending directly to you. For me, this image was just more love coming through from my Spirit Guides, and I am humbled by it and beyond grateful for it.

Around this time, I had an impulse to visit a local wellness center that offered meditation, yoga, and so forth. I chose one clinic, but I had the strangest experience with it, it was like I was being blocked from really making any solid connections with the team that ran the center. The first time I attempted to pop in was on a Saturday when it was supposed to be open, but the door was locked. About a year later, I went to their new location and got inside this time, but there was no one in the building for me to speak with; it was so bizarre! I had a sneaking suspicion that Spirit was doing the blocking, and no amount of questioning, cussing, or pleading would cause them to budge; later I knew that they had other plans for me. Sure enough, Spirit allowed me to go down another path; cue the dramatic spaghetti splat sounds!

While working on my computer one day I "stumbled" onto a video by a woman I had visited before for reflexology; in the video she was interviewing a local medium named Sharon. I heard this woman's story about the loss of her son and subsequent etheric connection with him and that was it, I had the urge to call and got her on the phone on my first attempt. I had no idea why I was seeking a conversation with a psychic medium, but there I was speaking with her. She began to tell me that she teaches people to become mediums, and all I could think of was, how the heck did I get here? It baffled me! Several weeks later, I found myself standing up in front of her group as she coached me through a basic conversation with Spirit. Sharon taught us the difference between being a psychic (they make predictions) and a medium (they connect with deceased loved ones). I honestly cannot remember the very moment when I connected to Spirit, but I do remember one of my most favorite readings I did during Sharon's class, it was for another member of the group. I asked Spirit to bring someone forward for the woman sitting in front of me, and in a flash, I saw a middle-aged, flamboyant performer dancing on stage wearing a top hat and fancy suit. It was incredible, and the woman sitting before me knew exactly who he was, holy crap!

As if that weren't enough, I felt another urge from Spirit to call Donna and ask if I could pay her to do some one-on-one training so that I could learn to communicate with Spirit. I found myself taking a crash course in how to speak with dead people! What the heck?! I had trained as a nurse, then worked in the pharmaceutical industry, and now I'm in medical devices, they are all rather structured areas of work, and it takes a lot of scientific understanding to do these jobs well. And, let's face it, it's one thing to dabble in visiting with psychics—a lot of people do that, and it can be interesting and sometimes fun. But "training" to be the one people go to for that kind of experience is not something you run to tell your colleagues about. I had my first big breakthrough during a one-on-one session with Donna, and even though we began by using tarot cards to get the etheric juices flowing, she snapped at me and said, "stop looking at the cards, tell me what you see." In a flash, I saw big red lips and mentioned a few other attributes about someone near and dear to her, and she responded with, "you're right!" I couldn't believe that I was connecting with Spirit!

I had yet another synchronistic encounter that year; yeah, you must know by now that Spirit was the driving force behind this one too. By this time, Peter and I were managing as best we could to create some sort of positive loving relationship, but I was definitely feeling a little worn out by the situation when one day, a very bubbly and handsome gentleman walked up to me in Walmart out of nowhere and said, "tell your man he's lucky to have you." Then about five minutes later, he returned and said, "tell him not to get complacent."

The Walmart Guy

While his messages resonated due to the ongoing challenges I was having with Peter, I began to wonder why Spirit would intersect me with this complete stranger. Would you believe that I bumped into this person at least four more times over the next few weeks, at other stores and even driving side-by-side one Saturday morning on my way to a hair appointment? It was ridiculous and yet noticeably clear that we were meant to connect. During that time, I had been dabbling a bit more in tarot cards and I'd even begun doing a few readings for others, but I would always preface my readings by saying that I wasn't particularly good at it. Anyway, after many run-ins with this man and mentions of my interest in tarot cards, he asked if I would do a reading for him. I was hesitant at first, but given the synchronicities surrounding our encounters, I agreed to meet *the Walmart guy* at a local restaurant after lunch; I did multiple readings for him over a bottomless cup of tea. We chatted more often after that, which moved the needle on our acquaintance status to a blossoming friendship. But later, I would come to know that this connection offered more, stay tuned!

During the third week of November 2017, I had an unexpected encounter while on an airplane that left me baffled. Back then, I had been flirting with the idea of writing a book, an idea that would probably never come to fruition. But this encounter left me smiling and shaking my head in disbelief; it was a blatant push from Spirit for me to write this book. So, here's what happened. I was sitting next to a rather demure and sophisticated-looking gentleman on a flight to Florida. I got a glimpse into his world, as I could hear the loud classical music playing on his headset. Near the end of the flight, we struck up a conversation and he revealed that he was an OBGYN (Obstetrics and Gynecology doctor) from Miami.

He proceeded to share a couple of things that were rather intriguing. The first was that as a doctor, he had delivered an international pop star into the world about three decades earlier; now I won't name drop here but trust me, you would be extremely impressed! Shortly thereafter, the doctor revealed that he was supposed to be on *The Oprah Winfrey Show*, another striking tidbit! Eventually, our conversation turned to metaphysics, and by the end of the flight, he stood up and mentioned something that caught me completely off guard, he said, "You're not normal, you need to find a way to get your message out." Then he handed me a pen with his name and clinic on it, grabbed his luggage, and walked off the plane. I was shocked and equally mesmerized by Spirit's emphatic nudge for me to take my journey with them more seriously. However, I had never written a book in my life, and as mentioned earlier, I truly couldn't stand reading during my teenage and young adult years; but my journey with Spirit gave me plenty of experiences to express on paper. Several months later, I tried to track that doctor down to ask if he would be interested in writing the foreword of my future book, but my attempts were futile, so I figured that it wasn't meant to be.

Anyway, on July 30, 2018, I poured makeup remover on a tissue and look at what emerged!

On Sept 26, 2018, more than a heart would appear before me! I completed an intuitive reading as a gift to a friend I had known since third grade. What's interesting is that many things that I was not privy to all those years ago were revealed throughout that session. She wrote a testimonial for which I am incredibly grateful, but the cool part can be found in the next image that I quickly snapped with my cellphone while speaking with her. The first image on the left was taken on another day prior to our session, simply because I loved how the reflection of the front door looked on the wall when the sun shone through it in the morning; note that I took the image while standing on the stairs. However, the second image to the right was captured during my debrief session with my friend over the phone. I was accustomed to making these calls with clients after I finished my channeled sessions alone with Spirit.

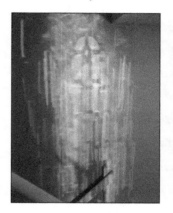

So, I was sitting on the couch when I looked up; I couldn't believe my eyes when I realized that an angel had appeared where the reflection of the door usually was. I snapped a shot as quickly as possible from my couch and immediately sent it to my friend's cellphone. I said to her, "this must be meant for you because I have never seen this image before in my home!" She could hardly believe it herself! We were talking about something that her loved one in spirit was disappointed with; and with that, she pointed out the frown at the top of the image; it was right on point with the message that had already come through. While I was completely mesmerized at the time; I'd have to say that nothing really surprises me when it comes to Spirit.

Here is the truly kind testimonial she provided after our session together:

A recent reading from Paula blessed me with such a gift...affirmation of life events, their meaning, along with their purpose served and placement in my journey moving forward. Such a profound experience with resonating, life-changing antidotes that can be summed up as I have come to understand that nothing ever goes away until it has taught us what we really need to know (and then some!). This is my first ever experience that I openly admit I have always wanted to do. I am so glad I did! Paula was able to not only validate life occurrences (that neither she nor others knew about) BUT provide a perspective and opportunity to reflect and interpret her readings. I am truly grateful for this opportunity and certainly feel blessed that Paula is using her God-given talent to make people's world a better place to work, live and play!

— D. B. (Ontario, Canada)

Reflection:

Mary Baker Eddy was right. Angels are thought to be gentle and feathery, and this one appeared as gently as it left. But that has not been my experience with Spirit Guides; they are a little more forthright when they are coming through. When I look back at the images of those hearts and the angel, I am taken right back to those awestruck moments, when my skeptical mind was converted even more. My Spirit Guides knew that I would need proof, and indeed they delivered. Yes, Spirit channels through everything, and they may even project their voice so you can hear them. So, quiet your mind, ask them to speak, then listen!

6

Signs, Symbols, & Synchronicities

*"Symbols are powerful because they are the
visible signs of invisible realities."*

~ SAINT AUGUSTINE (374–430)

A picture is worth a thousand words, and it is a very primitive yet effective way to communicate with others, as long as its meaning is understood. Earlier, I mentioned that the street sign, building name, and license plate, which I saw during my supernatural initiation with Wilson, appeared like modern-day hieroglyphics, and I felt compelled to interpret them; the same was true for those five hearts and the angel. It is interesting to note that hieroglyphics represent a style of communication through symbols which dates as far back as 5,000 years ago.[12] When I think about communication through languages, I am amazed by the diverse sounds and written expressions that exist around the globe. While living in Japan, I did my best to navigate around the city, but quickly realized that their stop signs, for instance, were different. A Japanese stop sign may be red and white like the North American version, but its triangular shape and Japanese writing threw me for a loop until I understood its meaning. It is clear that signs carry valuable information. Of course, body language is an effective form of communication as well—because nothing says, *get the bleep out of my way* like a flip of the middle finger from an aggressive driver, am I right?!

But seriously, there are innumerable ways to communicate using our five senses, and the ability to communicate is inherent in all living things: like birds, plants, and whales.

But what about non-living things? After a multitude of experiences with signs, symbols, and synchronicities from the supernatural realm, I developed an awareness that everything is "alive" on an atomic level, inherently telepathic, and can become animated into our physical world. Furthermore, I believe that signs, symbols, and synchronicities transit through the atomic level, by way of an "atomic superhighway". Imagine Spirit pulling over along the side of the road to pick you and another passenger up; hence a three-way interconnection is formed. I refer to this type of energetic communication with Spirit as our Universal language, and a key feature is its high vibrational frequency, which transcends all boundaries and synchronizes all into oneness. Remember, there is no 'I' in *Team*.

For humans, this language requires our five senses, advanced awareness through our sixth sense, and receptivity among other things, to fluently communicate with Spirit, and they are waiting for you to become aware of them: they're like, Yoo Hoo I'm over here! In the previous chapter, I shared some of those *Yoo Hoo* moments when I became aware of those five hearts and the angel. I concur with Saint Augustine's sage wisdom because I have come to appreciate that signs, symbols, and synchronicities are physical expressions of the supernatural realm; and they function much like hieroglyphs do to create a "sentence" that enables our interactions to take place. Moreover, Spirit enjoys this form of communication with us.

However, I didn't fully appreciate signs, symbols, and synchronicities from the etheric realm until my grand awakening with *Spirit, Wilson, and me*. It taught me that we can become energetically entangled with all that exists in the physical and non-physical realms. Before my initiation, I wasn't even consciously aware of Spirit, let alone communicating with these invisible entities; I was just going about life and talking to God in those days. My soul contract to channel the invisible realm was hidden deep within the recesses of my subconscious mind, until my awakening and spiritual discoveries through a series of destined soul lessons and other synchronous events. Earlier, I shared the profound experience which began on January 14, 2016, when Spirit lassoed Peter to form that trio bond. This interconnection was a Eureka for sure! It taught me that we can become energetically entangled with another person through our heart center and even with inanimate objects, like a car.

Then on February 16, 2017, I was bestowed the advanced awareness of clairaudience through the energetic entanglement between *Spirit, Rosepetal, and me.* I didn't see the heart sign sitting in the middle of the dining room table until I heard her shout, "Can you see it? Can you see it?" This experience with Rosepetal became etched in my mind and heart forever, and affirmed my belief that communication with Spirit is most certainly bidirectional. Even more, I realized that our Spirit Guides perform like puppeteers, working with precision to orchestrate synchronicities, which transit through the "atomic superhighway" and make contact with us. Spirit's "sleight of hand" with synchronicities is magical indeed, and you know it by the feeling it evokes in you; it's typically a *Wow!*

Sometime in 2017, a friend encouraged me to visit another tarot card reader who was quite an elderly lady. During our session, she told me that I would meet a Libra man and we'd know instantly that we were meant to come together and marry soon after. Both predictions were unshakeable, like they were pinned to my aura somehow; but in hindsight, I can tell you that the Turkish coffee reader and this gifted elderly woman were right! At the time I was delighted to take the next steps toward the opportunities that Spirit put in front of me as I tried to envision what was on its way in.

I am sure that everyone has had a *Wow* moment or two that defies logical explanation, but in this chapter, I will share how you can have more of them by expanding your awareness and perception of the ordinary, and when you do that, more of the extraordinary unfolds. This is how you do it!

Give Gratitude

I recommend starting by giving gratitude for your five senses which help to integrate us into our surroundings. Our five senses utilize the conscious and subconscious mind to help us navigate our dense earthly home. Meanwhile, our sixth sense utilizes the conscious and subconscious mind to help us navigate our luminous universal home. So, what does that mean? Well, communication with Spirit through your intuitive sixth sense is as organic as the language you were born to speak; therefore, you can use your sixth sense to communicate effortlessly with Spirit.

I suspect you have heard about the psychic senses reflecting our advanced perception through the Clairs;[13] here are some common terms used to describe them:

- clairvoyance (see)
- clairaudience (hear)
- clairsentience (feel)
- clairalience (smell)
- clairgustance (taste)
- claircognizance (know)

Your Spirit Guides know how to get your attention, but I encourage you to be open to receiving messages through all of the Clairs to foster these abilities. Note that there are an infinite number of tools to help you develop your sixth sense (AKA advanced awareness/perception); however, I have listed only a handful of them here, ultimately, you will need to discover which tools resonate most with you.

The first tool that can assist in the development of your sixth sense to communicate with Spirit is a divination card deck such as tarot or Lenormand. Secondly, your imagination is an extremely effective tool that you can utilize to interact with Spirit; pretend that you are communicating telepathically with them. Telepathy is the "*direct transference of thought from one person (sender or agent) to another (receiver or percipient) without using the usual sensory channels of communication...*"[14] Thirdly, visualization can help you create a more immersive experience with the invisible realm; and finally, I recommend that you pay attention to your dreams because Spirit can send precognitive solutions which can help in your awakened state.

Many stories are being shared about supernatural experiences that people are having through NDEs, something so mainstream now that it has its own acronym. And there are limitless accounts of people contacting aliens—and UFO disclosures have become "a thing."

So far, I've highlighted communication that can occur between living and non-living things through energetic entanglements, like trio bonds. Additionally, I mentioned a handful of tools from an infinite list of ways to speak with Spirit; so, let's take a deeper dive into how I interpret signs, symbols, and synchronicities, starting with a heart-shaped sign as an example. The meaning of a heart as a sign is straightforward, and I think you will agree that it is pretty universal; in my case, I was being showered with love from Spirit, which was exhilarating! However, when you hear someone use the expression that "something is a sign," they are referring to it as a foreshadowing of something to come.

Now, let's consider what those heart-shaped signs symbolized at the time for Paula. Notice how I time-stamped and personalized it? A symbol can have more than one personalized meaning which evokes an instant emotion; our emotions are energetic powerhouses, they can take us way up or way down in a heartbeat, and those extremes can make for some great song lyrics, as we all know. But here's the good news, you can control your emotions, and when you ask for help, your Spirit Guides can send tailored signs, symbols, and synchronicities, with impeccable timing to quell your emotions, and swell your excitement instead! There is no such thing as an impenetrable wall to Spirit, and yes, they see everything behind closed doors. Your Guides have access to all the information necessary to reach you; and their presence is enhanced by a simple request.

Anyway, over the course of a few years, as shown in the previous images, I was thankful for my Spirit Guide's endless love through heart-shaped signs materializing before me, but symbolically, hearts represented two diametrically opposing emotions. On one hand, I felt alive, animated, and supercharged by my connection with Spirit; but on the other hand, I was in a perpetual pattern of heartbreak trying to find my future husband, and I whined to Spirit about it incessantly. Over time, however, those heart-shaped signs would eventually symbolize so much more than the giddy emotion I felt by Spirit's love (good feels), and my impatience for a romantic life partner (bad feels). What do I mean? The symbol of a heart-shaped sign would morph into unimaginable realities, all of which posed as synchronicities to provide meaningful lessons for my soul's growth; as various references to the *heart* took center stage in my life.

Filled with Heart-Related Content

It wasn't until most of this book was written that I finally realized it was filled with heart-related content; take my Precious Moments figurine, for instance. Unbeknownst to me when I bought the

figurine, it would become a sign and a foreshadowing of Rosepetal and my work as a healer. While
her heart-filled headband represented the countless
hearts I received from Spirit; the palm of her hand
facing the world is what I literally do to help others
with my hands! Additionally, my physical heart's arrythmia in 2016 is another heart-related lesson from
Spirit, highlighting human energetic entanglements
through the heart center that can happen between
two people. The synchronicity with the OBGYN on
a flight to the US was a foreshadowing of the cardiac
surgeon who would ultimately write the foreword of
Fruit Fly Intelligence; however, Spirit provided another mind-blowing lesson through that interconnection as well. Before we dive in further, I want
to remind you that a synchronicity reflects, "*… the
happening by chance of two or more related or similar
events at the same time.*"

Later in this chapter, I will walk you through a basic approach that can assist with interpreting signs,
symbols, and synchronicities that you may encounter. Please note that the energetic language of the
Universe is highly personalized for each of us; and is
therefore infused through your Personal Navigation
System (PNS). Before we begin, I recommend that
you relax your logical mind, release all judgements,

be patient with yourself, and telepathically ask your Spirit Guides to open a protective channel of communication with you. Now, try this exercise to get your etheric juices flowing. I suspect that you would have come across the memorable black-and-white optical illusion of an old woman/young woman at some point in your life. I think I was first introduced to it back in grade school; but as I was writing the book, I became curious about its origin and found out some fascinating information:

"The famous Old Woman Young Woman optical illusion first appeared on a German postcard in 1888. However, its enduring popularity was instigated by the British cartoonist William Ely Hill, who adapted the image and published the illusion under the title "My Wife and My Mother-in-Law" in Puck magazine in 1915."[15]

For starters, perhaps the mention of these women may already be resonating with you. Stay open and objective. Anyway, let's keep going. I have chosen this optical illusion to demonstrate a simple approach to reading the subtleties, beyond seeing two women. It's imperative to observe and notice the subtleties of sign, symbols, and synchronicities which are steeped in everything around us; you'll find boundless information this way. For those who are tarot enthusiasts, you may appreciate that our environment is like one great big tarot card reading, and the messages vary depending on where you place your focus. For those who have not dabbled in the mystical arts before, it will be important to realize that what's gleaned from these subtleties will be most relevant to the seeker of the information, and your first impression is key.

I learned early on as I was going through my spiritual awakening to pause, quiet the mind, and observe everything objectively with all my senses—just take it all in. I continue this practice today, and in so doing, my feelings of curiosity, wonderment, and gratitude seem to pull me instantly into a trance-like state. That is when I am able to notice the subtleties of shapes, patterns, colors, timing, and so much more that are available through signs, symbols, and synchronicities. They come to me in pop-art-like fashion; like the license plate I saw during my initiation with Wilson. I can hear the world around me with greater sensitivity to receive messages relayed through songs, conversations, and more; the information is pulled into my ears by Spirit. And the sixth sense infused through our ears can sound as powerfully gripping as a marching band trampling through the brain. I can feel my body being touched, pressed, or needled by Spirit, seriously! Spirit makes physical contact with my body to validate visits from the other side; tastes and smells may be emphasized as well.

It is imperative that you be open to receiving messages through all five senses, but here's the best part: your physical senses don't even have to work! That's right! Spirit can send telepathic messages through your sixth sense by circumventing the other five. Your sixth sense knows exactly how to intuit spiritual information that is meant specifically for you (AKA your PNS). Case in point, I see orbs with my physical eyes mostly on the right, and I see images with my intuitive eye (AKA third eye), whether my eyes are opened or closed. Furthermore, my grown children have complained about my poor hearing, but despite some impairment, I feel I have managed just fine. In October 2022, I decided to have a test done by an audiologist to see what was going on. She followed up by email with the following explanation, but wishes to remain anonymous:

"Paula Marucci presents with a profound high frequency hearing loss in her right ear, and normal high frequency hearing in her left ear. Conversely, there is a more significant low frequency hearing loss in her left ear compared to her right ear. This configuration of hearing loss is fairly unusual. Typically, we see the

*same degree of hearing loss between the right and left
ears. During the appointment, Paula's ability to communicate did not seem to be impacted to the degree
that would be expected based on the severity of her
hearing loss."*

The point is that despite imperfect hearing, I can
hear Spirit in the field around my right side, rather
than through my right ear. It is my belief that every
human being on this planet can actively and passively receive spiritual messages, along with streams of
information through telepathic downloads, whether
the individual has compromised senses or not, and
whether they are aware of it or not.

Back to the exercise. The following list of questions have been chosen to get your intuitive juices
flowing, but keep in mind that you can ask an un-
limited number of questions. So, find a quiet space
and...

1. Be open
2. Breathe in and out peacefully
3. Surrender to flow
4. Lower your gaze
5. Observe the body and your surroundings
6. Express gratitude mentally (telepathy)

7. Ask whomever you pray to if they could press on your body so you can feel their loving touch. Notice the slightest touch, it's subtle!

8. Ask for a sign that is inexplicably yours; as I was writing this sentence, a fruit fly flew into my view, thanks Spirit!

9. Gently gaze and pay attention to things that you would normally ignore; acknowledge them and give them thanks for being with you on your journey. This is how you change your perception! Ask them a question and let your "mind" answer effortlessly; Spirit is often responding!

10. Observe yourself perceiving your surroundings differently

11. Did you notice colors, patterns, timing, and so forth?

12. Was there something that resonated within *Fruit Fly Intelligence?* Layer that onto this exercise and see if you can garner information about the answers you seek

13. Get excited for your next sign, symbol, and synchronicity!

14. String them together to get a message from Spirit

15. Spirit is already communicating with you, so you should be better equipped to notice and, once you do, you will feel exhilaration! Harness that energy by staying upbeat (supercharged-quickening feels)

16. Don't forget to write them down!

Reflection:

It wasn't until my initiation with *Spirit, Wilson, and me,* that I learned to take signs, symbols, and synchronicities seriously; now I consider them sacred because they are powerful messages from an invisible force. These invisible realities are "alive" on an atomic level, inherently telepathic, and can become animated into our physical world in the blink of an eye; they can manifest in infinite ways. Because of this, I have come to appreciate that we are one with the Universe, a part of its natural rhythm and flow, like the sound of a heartbeat, or a bird's song, or the ebb and flow of the ocean. So, pay attention to the world around you, for it is alive and filled with meaningful messages that are waiting for you to discover them.

7

Sprinkling Pixie Dust

"The moment one definitely commits oneself, then
Providence moves too. Whatever you think you
can do, or believe you can do, begin it.
Action has magic, power, and grace.
~ JOHANN WOLFGANG VON GOETHE (1749–1832)

Sharon the psychic medium saw me sprinkling pixie dust during a personal reading with her around 2017. I was so moved by this message that I decided to reference it on my first psychic medium business card (yes, we're professionals, too). The card has a blue, white, and green image of the top of the earth with a fairy hovering above, and she is scattering pixie dust all over the world. The craziest thing is that it started to play out that way for real! While hearts were floating in and out of my life, so too were people I'd never met before. It is noteworthy that I am not a fan of writing my thoughts, feelings, opinions, and experiences down on paper, yet I am writing this book because Spirit wants me to share

their magnificence with you. I often forget messages
I have channeled for others; but those I am meant to
share have stickability, as if scribed within the cir-
cuit of my heart and mind instead.

In March of 2018, I was at an all-day meeting
for work in medical devices, when I felt the urge to
quickly touch base with *the Walmart guy*, who by this
time had become a friend. My pull to text him was
timely because I learned that he'd just undergone
bilateral eye surgery and was in a fair bit of pain.
I had never been to his house before, but I offered
to pop by and hover my hands over his eyes with
the intention of easing his discomfort. I informed
him that I would connect with my Guides, hover
my hands for about five-to-ten minutes, then touch
his feet to ground him at the end of the session; and
with that he granted me permission. The next morning, he texted to say that although he normally had
trouble sleeping, especially while in pain, he ended
up having one of the best sleeps he'd had in a while.

However, the day after I hovered over *the Walmart
guy's* eyes, I remember waking up with a bit of a buzz,
not from alcohol, but from that powerful supercharged-quickening (and now buzzy) feeling that I
get when connecting with Spirit. I figured that spiritual "pixie dust" must have flowed through my hands

in *both* directions—to his physical eyes, resulting in a more comfortable and fitful sleep, and to my mind's (intuitive) eye, which resulted in an increase in the speed of my previous channeling ability. Through this upgrade, my reception of spiritual messages became instantaneous! With that exchange of energy between us, I am being reminded to share the apex purpose of *Fruit Fly Intelligence,* which is this:

The relationships we cultivate in our lives with all that exists in the physical and non-physical realms bring more value than the eyes can see; for we are dynamically interconnected beings that vibrate with the life force of Source energy; knowing this leads to an extraordinary life!

Anyway, after our session, I developed an insatiable urge to get channeling! It was like I needed to discharge my battery to gain balance within my body because of this pent-up, buzzy energy; and with Spirit on recharge duty, I'd be ready to channel again when the urge peeked. These impromptu "Jack-in-the-box" channeling moments would go on for about two years until the insatiable urge to channel for strangers finally dissipated.

So, on March 9th, with the spiritual buzz moving through me, I drove to a doctor's appointment, got settled in the examining room, and waited for the physician to arrive. But then a nurse I hadn't met before walked into the room. In that moment, I felt the urge to introduce myself, then blurted out that I'm a psychic medium; I asked if she'd like a message; got her permission, and instantly saw pieces of metal. I asked what the significance could be, and she said, "oh, I had titanium placed in my ankle a few months ago." I thought, oh wow, I didn't see that coming!

Now, the next sequence of events is a bit of a blur because I was in an *eat-sleep-channel-repeat* phase, as Spirit urged me to walk up to strangers wherever they were to provide messages. I'd start each conversation by introducing myself and sharing what I do, and then I'd ask if the person wanted a reading. I'd wait for permission, and almost everyone responded with a resounding, "yes!" These experiences were wonderous for the people I was reading for, and even for me because the validations of accuracy reported back were astounding! It kept that buzzy feeling alive inside, which in turn fueled the insatiable urge to continue channeling. It's as if Spirit had ordered spiritual community service for me to complete; I was giving back to others in such a loving and healing way, and it was an absolute honor and privilege to do so.

On one occasion, I was sitting in a local restaurant waiting to place my order when I got the sudden urge to share my psychic ability. So, once the server arrived, I introduced myself, gave my pitch, asked for permission, and in a flash, I saw a man's hand in a white glove. He was shaking Christmas bells, and so I asked the server what the significance could be, and she replied, "oh, well, I was born on Christmas Day." I shook my head in disbelief and quietly thanked Spirit for the information. A few other messages came through, which I can no longer recall, after which I finished my meal, paid the bill, and then off I went.

I was flying quite a bit for work at this time and often found myself in airports, hotels, and restaurants, which gave this channeler the perfect playground to work in. On one occasion, I was sitting in an airport restaurant, and we all know how busy they can be. So, with the buzz fueling my urge to channel, I introduced myself to a woman, gave my pitch, asked for permission, and in the next moment, I heard Spirit whisper, *she's pregnant*. When I shared this, she looked stunned and asked, "How could you know? I'm only three months pregnant and no one at work knows about it." Then she said, "I am so worried about this baby, will it be alright?" In a flash, I saw the sweetest little girl, dressed in pink, sitting upright with legs crossed and leaning toward me; she was all smiles. Oh, my goodness, *I* was tickled pink just seeing this little cutie! I proceeded to share my vision with the expectant mother and watched the stress melt off her face. It felt so good to help ease her worries. I finished my breakfast, paid the bill, and headed toward the gate to catch my flight.

There was yet another person who Spirit wanted me to speak with, only this time, the gentleman was a staff member at a hotel in California where I was staying for business. We exchanged pleasantries on the first day, however, I saw him again early the next morning and felt the buzz from Spirit. So, I shared what I do, gave my pitch, asked for permission, and in a flash, I saw a sophisticated-looking man in my mind's eye. The hotel employee standing before me knew exactly who he was and was thrilled to be hearing from his father. I can only remember a few messages from that session, but the main takeaway, which baffled me personally, is how our imagination factors into connecting with the spirit realm. I will need to share a purchase I made for you to appreciate the message that came through for this hotel employee. About five years earlier, I had been shopping at a local furniture store when I fell in love with a 50" x 50" print of a white Siberian tiger. *She* looks as large as life, and so I felt the urge to quietly give her a name, which seemed rather fanciful for a grown woman to do, but with Spirit, there is always a reason; her name is Tika.

Who is Tika?

So, during this impromptu reading in the hotel lobby, Spirit flashed an image of this print of my white Siberian tiger, and I blurted out, who is Tika? The man before me was shocked and proceeded to share that it was his deceased father's pet name for his sister. I was dumbfounded! This reading cemented my belief that our imagination is an active doorway to the unseen world. Below is the lovely testimonial I received on December 6, 2018, from the hotel associate about our session together with Spirit. He wrote:

What a beautiful Thanksgiving week. Something that my mother and siblings never experienced before. I met Paula by chance encounter, after a few words of pleasantries our conversation turned towards the unexplainable only a few would understand. When Paula confirmed my willingness to have an open mind, she shared with me her wonderful gift. I was amazed at the accuracy of what she shared with me, imagine a complete stranger who lives 3,000 miles away would tell me intimate details that only our family keep to ourselves. Paula has a gift that could bring joy to families...my sister was in tears and my mother was completely amazed by the message from our departed father. Even the pet name my father calls my sister was used to deliver his message. Paula has a special gift that I hope she would use to bring some closure or to reconnect with departed loved ones. I am very thankful and grateful to the joy she gave to our family.

— B. (California)

The next reading was quite different and a bit of a doozy, because while I was at this same hotel in the US on business, in my mind's eye over the course of a week I kept seeing a little boy and a man, who I assumed to be the boy's father. I really didn't pay much attention at first, but eventually heard the little boy in spirit say, *"I wanna speak to my mama."* Shortly after that, and with the spiritual buzz moving through me, I walked up to an acquaintance I'd met years earlier, shared what I do, gave my pitch, and then asked for permission to share what I'd been experiencing. She looked like a deer caught in headlights upon hearing the information, then repositioned herself as tears welled up in her eyes. Apparently, it was her partner who died years ago, and he was coming through with the baby they never had together. As a channeler, I have come to understand that while the body has a shelf life; the essence of a being never dies. Later, she shared that our conversation was healing and therapeutic for her, and all I could think was *oh, thank goodness*!

As time passed, I continued doing these "Jack-in-the-box" style readings, but they became fewer and far between, and that transition seemed to happen organically. I guess my community service had been a success because my impromptu sessions morphed into more scheduled readings which I began charging a fee for. During these scheduled sessions, I would take a more methodical approach to call in my Spirit Team and placed a perpetual request for protection as I navigated through the etheric realm. I was amazed by the amount of accurate and granular details that I was able to retrieve in this way, and the healing that came through for my clients was astounding!

In time Spirit brought me face-to-face with an individual I will call Sandy. The trio bond formed here made me aware of Spirit's touch, to serve as validation of a visit from the spirit realm. Here is what happened: I was sitting across from Sandy's desk when I felt the urge to share that I was a psychic medium, then gave my pitch, asked for permission, and instantly felt pressure over my entire chest; Sandy knew exactly who the visitor was from the spirit realm. I was utterly shocked that Spirit could access my body in this way, and to be honest, it freaked me out! Even though Sandy was excited to hear more from this visitor, I personally needed time to gather my composure. So, I decided to complete the channeling piece at home alone with my Spirit Guides, then followed up via text with Spirit's message. I shook my head in disbelief as I read the incredibly warm testimonial that Sandy sent on December 3, 2018:

'I have had readings performed in the past for close loved ones that unfortunately left me questioning the validity of the encounter, resulting in me reading into claims to validate, never fulfilling my needs to know what I always wanted to. I had known Paula for a few years and discovered through some casual conversation that she had been performing readings recently. I asked if she would consider performing one for myself about a close friend that had passed that I often thought of and wondered if he had felt the same close relationship that I did (best buds)? Paula immedi-

ately accepted my request and at that moment felt the presence of my friend. Paula revealed to me what she was experiencing, and I knew she was connected to him. Paula later performed her connection in private with my friend and revealed the results later to me. To say the least, I was floored with her findings. I was literally shaking and emotional as I felt his presence when reading through Paula's encounter. Everything fit perfectly, all of my curiosities—wanting to know if we shared the same thoughts—were answered with no need to read into Paula's findings. I was able to explain and validate back to Paula that her experiences were totally accurate and truly amazing, as only my friend and I shared these connections. I can't thank Paula enough for coming into my life and connecting me with my "Best Bud" who has been gone now for thirty years. Paula you are truly gifted, and I thank you for sharing your gift with me!'

— S. F. (Ontario, Canada)

The next channeling experience I had involved a lovely gentleman I met through my mother. We spoke for a few minutes on this particular occasion, then I shared what I do, asked for permission, and in the next moment, I heard a grandfather-like energy in spirit whistling a song with the word green in it.

I shared this with the man before me, who looked puzzled, because he wasn't sure who was whistling from the other side. The grandfather-like spirit relayed a message about a specific elderly family member. Then my mom's friend left but called a few days later to share that he had spoken with his mother, and she validated that it was indeed his grandfather coming through, even the whistling part about a song with the word green in it, which was a thing he had often done. Eventually, this family friend followed his grandfather's advice and was able to heal an emotional wound before the death of the elderly member occurred.

Gray Locks and a Vibrant Personality

On another occasion, I was sitting in a local restaurant with a friend and waiting to place our order, by now you know that I love to eat out. Anyway, a waitress whom I had never met before approached the table bursting with cheeriness, so I introduced myself, gave my pitch, asked for permission, and in a flash, I saw a grandfather-like energy with gray locks and a vibrant personality, he walked toward me and whacked me on the forehead, but I instantly knew that it was meant for the waitress. I shared this with her, and she looked at me like I had three heads;

admittedly, I felt a bit embarrassed because that was all I could glean from Spirit.

This reading occurred in the fall of 2019, but around February 2020, I went back to the same restaurant with my teenage daughter and saw this waitress again. She wasn't serving our table this time, but walked up to me and said, "I was speaking with my aunt about you a few weeks ago and she [aunt] almost fell on the floor." So, I wondered if I had predicted a fall with the whack to the forehead vision I'd seen. Then the server proceeded to share that her aunt informed her that the man who came through in spirit was indeed the waitress' grandfather; he apparently was known to walk up to people at family functions, whack them on the forehead, and say, "don't you wish you had a V8?" I shook my head in disbelief and quietly thanked Spirit for validating the bizarre reading we had done the previous fall. We finished our meal, I paid the bill, and then off we went.

The final reading that I will share to bookend some of my "Jack-in-the-box" sessions occurred during the pandemic. I was sitting in the St. John's International airport restaurant feeling tired and hungry when I saw a man sitting alone next to me. Telepathically, I told Spirit that I wasn't in the mood and said, *if you want me to channel then make it obvious*. The next thing I knew I was introducing myself, gave my pitch, asked for permission, then spilled a bunch of details about his life, his wonderful wife, and children which I can't even recall; but what I do remember is that he was full of emotion as I witnessed him smiling, then tear up from the information that Spirit wanted me to share. After that, I finished my meal, paid the bill, and headed toward the gate to catch my flight.

As I finished writing this chapter of *Fruit Fly Intelligence*, I realized that I'd have some 'splainin to do, but before that, I'd need to find a way to understand it all for myself first. Let me start by laying my personal foundational discovery that Spirit channels through everything, because everything is connected with Source energy; more pointedly, everything *is* Source energy. Remember, when you look into the eyes of family, friends, frenemies, and fruit flies, who do you think is staring back at you? *Hi Source!*

Okay, in keeping with the "pixie dust" theme, my big question is, how does Spirit work through my body and urge me to open my mouth to "sprinkle pixie dust" in the form of loving messages and healing energy onto others? From my point of view, I suspect that these transmissions involve concepts way beyond my comprehension, but I feel drawn to electrons to help me explain it. Electrons are *"one of the three basic subatomic particles—along with protons and neutrons—that make up atoms, the basic building blocks of all matter and chemistry."*[16] Atoms are the building blocks of both living and non-living things, which therefore includes human cells. Remember the atomic superhighway I mentioned earlier? After a multitude of supernatural experiences with signs, symbols, and synchronicities, I developed an awareness that everything is "alive" on an atomic level, inherently telepathic, and capable of becoming animated into the physical world. Look at me getting all scientific when I haven't got a frigging clue what I'm talking about!

Anyway, I wonder if those supercharged-quickening-buzzy feels that I get when I am trio-bonded with Spirit and another person as I channel messages, have something to do with electrons (AKA electricity) moving through my nervous system *and* heart (Spirit says the heart is the human portal) acting like a conductor wire which tunes me in (like a radio station) to the work I do for Spirit. I am envisioning myself as a potato battery, where a chemical reaction creates an electrical charge, stop laughing![17]
"Our cells are specialized to conduct electrical currents.

Electricity is required for the nervous system to send sig-nals throughout the body and to the brain [and heart], making it possible for us to move, think, and feel."[18]

You may recall when I shared earlier in the book that I had experienced an "outage" of sorts as a child which required yearly electroencephalograms (EEGs) to ensure that all was well with the electrical activity of my brain; some might say that my brain is not firing on all cylinders, but that's a topic for an-other book. Furthermore, I shared that I thought I'd had a heart attack in 2016 which necessitated a few electrocardiograms (ECGs) to check the electrical signals of my heart. Both events were orchestrated by Spirit; my brain got a surge in energy which re-sulted in my drop to the floor, and my heart got a surge in energy which manifested in the form of an arrythmia, both steered me into a series of soul les-sons. So, let's use these electrical events as a jump-off point into the topic of electromagnetic energy. Wait, *what*?! Fun fact: *"The heart is the most powerful source of electromagnetic energy in the human body, producing the largest rhythmic electromagnetic field of any of the body's organs. The heart's electrical field is about sixty times greater in amplitude than the electrical activity generated by the brain."[19]*

Remember Pig-Pen?

So, what does this even mean? To help you envision an electrical field, think of Pig-Pen from the comic strip Peanuts.[20] He is always seen in a cloud of dust, but instead of dust, imagine everything being surrounded by colorful energy (AKA your aura), which transcends space and time. This luminous electrical energy surrounds our physical body to create an electrical field, and this field has magnetic properties, making it electromagnetic. It's your electromagnetic field (EMF) that initially makes contact with others, especially those for whom you have an affinity. Then you can walk up to the cutie across the room and say "heyyy!" That's right, blame it on your EMF for making you so naughty, just kidding! Here is the takeaway: we are drawn to (and repel) others for countless reasons; and our electromagnetic field is sensitive to that. This is the energy which interconnected me with Spirit and those trio bonds that I have highlighted here in *Fruit Fly Intelligence*. I can instantly connect with Spirit telepathically to help others, it's just like tuning into a station on the radio.

I recently asked my Spirit Guides to help me understand more about these "pixie dust" interconnections between *Spirit, others, and me*, and this is what they said:

We have boundless benevolent ways of connecting with humans, to answer your question Paula, we go through your heart space, the "I love" portal if you will.

After I heard their explanation, I found myself listing a myriad of things that I love, here we go:

- I love my children
- I love Source
- I love my Spirit team
- I love Mother Earth (AKA Gaia) and her colors
- I love my soul family
- I love my DNA family
- I love my friends
- I love my home
- I love freedom
- I love water
- I love warmth
- I love whales, and cats
- I love creativity
- I love Kicking Horse coffee
- I love bread
- I love basil
- I love cilantro
- I love garlic
- I love cinnamon
- I love pasta

- I love wine
- I love culture
- I love languages
- I love travel
- I love music
- I love Mei-lan
- I love Barbra Streisand
- I love RuPaul (and Jinkx Monsoon, and Ms. Cracker, and Jujubee, and Aquaria, and Monét X Change; not you Michelle Visage, just kidding, love you too)
- I love Dr. Elisa Medhus (and Erik)
- I love Dominique Sachse (girl power!)
- I love to laugh
- I love Jim Carrey
- I love Jim Gaffigan
- I love Iliza Schlesinger
- I love Wanda Sykes
- I love Celeste Barber
- I love Keanu Reeves, *heyyy*
- I love Japanese taiko drumming
- I love fruit flies (big surprise)

It could take days to list all of the people, places, and things for which I am grateful. To all, I say a heartfelt THANK YOU for your contribution to the world! Just ordinary stuff, right? Well, when you *feel* it with gratitude, it increases your vibrational frequency, which attracts more synchronicities, taking your life from ordinary to extraordinary! That's it! That's what's been priming me to connect with Spirit and feel their surge in the form of those super-charged-quickening-buzzy feels that I get; it's gratitude ya'll! Gratitude is the grand electron, at least in my case. It literally raises your vibrational frequency which intrinsically raises your consciousness. That is how you get more out of life! I am often in a state of gratitude and wonderment, and I thank Source and my Spirit Team on a daily basis for the abundance I enjoy around me.

30 Minutes of Love

Try this exercise. Write down everything that you love, well, not everything, because that could take all day, but set a timer for about thirty minutes and jot down things that you love. But don't write, "I love herbs" if they don't evoke a high vibrational emotion from you (you have to *give* in this way to *receive*); balance is important. And instead of just writing what you love, highlight the item's color, aroma, taste, availability, and so forth; add everything about it that *moves* you. Notice how this exercise makes you *feel*; that's powerful energy right there! Harness it by staying upbeat to attract more high-vibe experiences. One more thing. I mentioned that electrons are one of the subatomic forces involved in those "pixie dust" transmissions, right? It turns out that they act like little wizards, changing their behavior when being observed versus when they are not. I bring this up because I wonder if their behavior had something to do with that shapeshift moment when I saw Wilson's smile over the GM's mouth. Quantum Physicists study the properties and behaviors of electrons. Check out The Double-Slit Experiment.[21] It's fascinating!

Anyway, some of those "pixie dust" moments made me question the purpose of life's challenges. But I began to understand that we are here on Earth to experience good, bad, and anything in between for the evolution of our soul; and that many of our lessons are predetermined before we're born. But we do have an element of free will and are therefore able to control the controllables, simply by making better choices. Our choices can determine where we land on that *good-to-bad continuum* of life experiences. That said, I do my best to see the good in all the experiences of my life; no matter how troubling they may be. Perceiving our world from the good corner of the continuum has its vibrational perks; it helps me stay upbeat and in better alignment to the magic that life has to offer.

If you are wondering what I mean by that, just think about your body posture and subsequent actions if you were told: "You have two weeks left to live," versus "You won $50,000,000!" In the former scenario, I imagine that hearing such devastating news would shock us awake, then slump us forward in despair. Yet, the latter would have us dancing the jig; so, control what you can and choose to keep dancing! Ultimately, I believe that my Spirit team deserves all the credit, along with loved ones who came through during these sessions; I am humbled and grateful to help others in this lifetime. Note that I am not privy to everything: when I am not permitted to know something, my Guides simply will not budge. To think that these "pixie dust" experiences began with an energetic interconnection between *Spirit, Wilson, and me.* Wow!

Reflection:

The quote from Johann Wolfgang von Goethe that began this chapter was both poetic and precise. My whole spiritual journey is the result of Providence moving through me, in the form of those supercharged-quickening-buzzy feels I get when inter-connected with Spirit and others, especially through trio bonds for destined soul lessons. This is not only available to me, but to everyone. And in my experi-ence, the electricity powered by gratitude helped me spread magical "pixie dust" to others. Spirit channels through all of us. Have you ever blurted something out and wondered, "where did that come from?". I believe that brilliant minds like Samuel Morse, Nikola Tesla, and Albert Einstein actively and/or passively downloaded their discoveries from Provi-dence. My downloads from Spirit to "sprinkle pix-ie dust" is not because I am special, it's simply my soul-contracted mission for this lifetime.

8

A Colorful Imagination

"A Man's life is dyed the color of his imagination."
~ MARCUS AURELIUS (121–180)

I had just finished a satisfying breakfast at a Denny's restaurant sometime in 2015, when I decided to use the washroom before heading out. After I had done my business I placed my hand under the automatic soap dispenser and became transfixed by the ocean blue light emanating from the device. Odd as it sounds, I couldn't move my gaze away. I eventually managed to wash my hands, and when I placed them under the automatic hand dryer, the same thing happened. You laugh, right? I was completely enchanted by the color and had no idea why! But I allowed myself to be fully present in that moment there in the Denny's washroom; I began to smile. Looking back, I realized that it was the same supercharged-quickening feeling as before, which instantly lifts my mood with excitement; the buzzy feels I get when Spirit is moving through me as I channel came later.

One day in early Spring of that year, I had another long-lasting moment with color while I was in the doctor's office waiting room. For some reason, that day, I decided to sit across from the super-sized aquarium I had thoughtlessly passed numerous times before. But on this sunny afternoon, I was drawn to look straight through it; and when I did, I saw a vast array of colors that appeared to paint the entire wall behind it; it was mesmerizing! I did my best to snap a shot of the image with my cellphone, but unfortunately, it did little justice, as the image only captured about fifty percent of what my eyes could see. The image I took was devoid of the beautiful bands of red that I saw with my physical eyes; however, the loveliest blue color made itself known. I felt another supercharged-quickening feeling during that moment.

Upon reflection, I realized I'd had a long-standing belief about the color blue that dates as far back as my childhood. For some reason, I felt that this color belonged to my sister. You see, it had been my sister's favorite color when we were young; I remember her bedroom wallpaper being filled with its essence. I, however, was drawn to shades of pink, which occasionally reflects in my choices as an adult. As an aside, I find it funny how old beliefs stick with us. I am not sure why I felt that the color blue belonged to my sister, it simply was the way my childhood mind perceived it. When I fast-forward to my more adventurous years as a teenager, the thought had faded away. It is important to understand the root cause of old beliefs and release that which no longer serves you. As for the color blue, well, it is absolutely one my favorites now, and for good reason too. Stay tuned!

Sometime in 2016, I had another unusual yet very profound experience with color when I caught a glimpse of my cat's aura: it flashed like a rainbow over his sweet little head when the sun beamed upon him just so; for me, seeing Marbles' aura was proof that we have an energetic body surrounding the physical one. And more importantly, that we are so much more than what our eyes can see. It appeared that Spirit had amplified my sense of sight to appreciate the colors of the rainbow in a more expansive and energetic way. Having this colorful experience with Marbles generated that supercharged-quickening feeling once again. Such bizarre lessons to learn, especially given that I am not a scientist, a biologist, a chemist, a quantum physicist, nor an interior decorator! But, apparently it didn't matter because my Guides forged ahead and schooled me in the field of spiritual energy, and colors were the next topic on their list; I continue to learn more every day. It was around this time that I created my business, which I called *The Intuition Studio*. It has taken many years to digest all these experiences in a way that allows me to share them coherently with you; and of course, I have asked my Spirit Guides for assistance as well.

As the years went by, I continued to have experiences with signs, symbols, and synchronicities from the supernatural realm; I concluded that everything is "alive" on an atomic level, inherently telepathic, and can become animated into our physical world. So, why would color be any different? When we see a rainbow in the sky after a rainfall, we usually see visible light, which is comprised of red, orange, yellow, green, blue, indigo, and violet. Light is energy (AKA electromagnetic radiation); it is made up of various wavelengths which we see as color, like the ones we see in a rainbow.[22] Blue light, which is of particular interest to me, "… *has a higher frequency and carries more energy than red light.*"[23]

Why is all this relevant for an energy channeler? Well, since light is energy, we can interact (interconnect) with it in the same way that Spirit did with me and others to create trio bonds; and supernatural forces are energy as well. The trio bonds which I have highlighted in *Fruit Fly Intelligence* are as natural as the bonds between hydrogen and oxygen atoms to form a molecule of water (H_2O); and they seem to associate and disassociate in the same way as well. I have come to understand that each of my previous experiences with color were orchestrated in order for me to have incremental electromagnetic upgrades; consequently, my vibration and subsequent frequency were being stretched like muscles in a Jane Fonda workout. Over time, I would see the result of my Spirit Guide's work and the benefit it would provide to others. Of course, I wasn't aware of this at the time, but it was on my soul's roadmap, if you will. Admittedly, I had to unpack the concepts of vibration and frequency to make sense of it all.

Simply put, a vibration is a back-and-forth motion;[24] for example, windshield wipers moving back and forth at low speed. Healthline describes vibrations as rhythms that happen in our body: *"Heartbeats, breathing rates, and circadian rhythms are examples of physiological rhythms we can see, feel, and measure."*[25] On a personal note, there have been a few occasions while standing on my mother's kitchen floor that I could feel a constant tremor beneath my feet; when I asked my family if they could feel it too, they would say, "no." I believe that I was able to detect the vibration of the furnace through the floor because I was becoming highly sensitive to the subtle vibrations in my environment.

Trouble Sleeping

Additionally, when I was living in a condo, I frequently had a doozy of a time trying to fall asleep because my body could sense the vibration coming from the nearby utility closet; the problem worsened if I had a few glasses of wine and a big meal. Okay so, then what is a frequency? It refers to how often that back-and-forth motion repeats per second and it is measured in hertz (Hz).[26] Keeping with the windshield wipers analogy, when they are running at high speed, we say they have a higher frequency. According to HealthandBass.com: *"...On a quantum level, everything is vibrating at various frequencies."*[27]

A few years ago, a bizarre incident occurred when I was having trouble with my garage door opening, so I asked Imants to come over and take a look at it for me. Imants was fully aware of my spiritual skills and thought he'd be funny and placed the voltage tester pen against my elbow. This is a portable device which is used to check for live wires prior to doing any electrical work; would you believe the red light started to flash! What the heck?! So, he tested his elbow a few times, and nothing happened.

Later, we discovered that pressing the voltage tester pen against my elbow while I was standing closer to my cell phone made the tester respond more readily. It was evident that the device was responding to my frequency which appeared to increase when it was energetically entangled (AKA interconnected) with my cellphone; in those moments, I was registering as a live wire! Given the title of this book, I feel it is appropriate to highlight that there is a vibrational frequency in fruit flies as well. *"... fruit flies can beat their wings about 250 times a second."*[28] Impressive right?!

In 2018, I was pulled into another connection with an individual that later turned out to be a trio bond; orchestrated by Spirit to teach us about the energetic power of color; this incident was nothing short of gob-smacking! Here's what happened. I bumped into a lovely woman I worked with in the pharmaceutical industry. We stood in the parking lot of a coffee shop for quite some time catching up with each other about work and life. I shared that I was single, which led to a conversation about her friend; it was around a week later when she introduced me to a cardiac surgeon named John. He and I met and dated briefly until something unimaginable happened with Spirit. It began one day when we were chatting about an old injury that he'd been dealing with.

So, I decided to share some information about energy healing, using the familiar term, "Reiki." However, I told him that I would not be using the Reiki techniques which I had learned years earlier. Instead, I would work with my Spirit Guides while hovering my hands over his hip; despite having zero confidence in my ability to help him, I felt drawn to do it anyway once he granted me permission. I turned to my Spirit Guides who took the lead, and in a flash, I saw the most magnificent color blue penetrating his hip. I gasped silently in amazement! Even more astounding was the verbal feedback I received from John the next day; I was shocked! He shared that he had experienced about "85% less pain" from our session together, then jokingly held his hands up for another zap! I asked if he would kindly write a testimonial. And later, it dawned on me to ask if he would consider writing the foreword of this book, and he agreed! Ever since my interaction on the plane with the OBGYN, I wished that I could find a credible individual to write the foreword for this book, and poof! Here he was! Ask and you shall receive! I thought I would share John's testimonial referencing that magical moment between *Spirit, John, and me,* which I received in April 2019:

As a surgeon I was trained to use science and precision in my work. However, experience taught me that there is so much more to healing than we know or understand. Although I have become very confident in my abilities, I also gained much humility. It is with this humility and an open mind that I was able to speak with Paula and learn about a whole different approach to life and healing. On a personal note, I was suffering from hip pain likely due to running. I had received physiotherapy with some success but there was still a significant amount of discomfort. Paula offered to do Reiki, which I had heard of but was very skeptical about in the past. With my new humble approach to life, I was non-judgmental and open to new ideas. Paula did a short ten-minute session during which I felt warmth over my hip. I started to walk around and noticed immediately that it was different. The discomfort wasn't completely gone, but it was significantly better and remained so to the point that I started to play hockey. As a doctor, I can't explain what happened. I do know there is more to healing than pills and surgery. It involves the mind and the heart. Paula can't perform miracles, but if you open up with your heart and mind without judgment it is amazing how she may be able to help you shape your life.
— JL (Ontario, Canada)

The experiences with John, Marbles, at Denny's, and the doctor's office were instrumental in helping me expand my awareness to include the concept of color as a formidably gripping energy that is able to carry healing properties. If Spirit brought the blue light to the party, then why was I needed? I believe it was for the transmission of the energy to occur. A transmitter can be defined as *"a person or thing [Paula's hands] that causes something [blue healing energy], to be spread or transmitted to others [John's hip]."*[29]

Our interconnection enabled the transfer of Spirit's blue healing energy, resulting in an unconventional form of pain relief. While this is a rather simplistic explanation for what took place during our session, it makes sense. Since this incredible event, I respectfully work with my Spirits Guides to incorporate colorful energy into my healing sessions with others when required to do so. I am so grateful when my clients report feeling relaxed, revitalized, and/or are experiencing a reduction in their pain. For example, in April 2019 I received the following kind words after another energy-healing session:

> *I had a recurring groin injury that was giving me so much discomfort that I was waking up with pain at night (initial injury happened a few years back). I*

also had a right shoulder tear in the tendon confirmed by ultrasound. Paula hovered over both sites for about ten minutes and the groin pain was gone after two days; Since then, I have gone running about five times and still no groin pain; the shoulder has improved. I never used to believe in this, but now I strongly recommend that anyone with pain see Paula.

— S.H. (Ontario, Canada)

Additionally, I have had several healing sessions while interconnected between *Spirit, Mom, and me*; unfortunately, she has been suffering with psoriatic arthritis. It's amazing how a five-to-ten-minute "zap" could take her pain away or at least diminish it. On a few occasions, I have witnessed her go from being slumped over in pain to smiling from ear to ear, and then she'd pop up from the chair to show off her ability to bend and dance; and that's after about a ten-minute zap! Spirit never ceases to amaze me. However, I've had to release my own disappointment when her pain would return days later, taking up residence in some other part of her body; and now she is responding even less, which is very unfortunate. I have had to accept that some people come into this lifetime with a soul contract of disease in place, and yet others create disease that does not have to be ex-

perienced. Either way, I had to learn to have com-
passion and release the outcome, it is simply none
of my business, I am merely a connection to Source
energy, that is all that I have been called to do.

Energy Healing is Not New!

Energy healing is not a new phenomenon, Reiki for
example, has been practiced for centuries.[30] And you
have likely heard about our beloved international
healer, Charlie Goldsmith. Charlie has been working to bring energy healing into mainstream conversations as an effective modality of healing. He
highlighted his ability on The Learning Channel's
(TLC) show, *The Healer,*[31] and participated in a hospital study featuring energy healing that showed very
favorable results. Please visit Charlie's website if you
would like to learn more about this study: https://
www.charliegoldsmith.com/.[32]

Light energy has been incorporated into various
treatment modalities for quite some time; for instance, light therapy is an option for people with sea-
sonal affective disorder (SAD).[33] Additionally, LED
light therapy is utilized in the medical aesthetics
field to treat various skin conditions such as acne and
psoriasis.[34] I am sure that there are a number of other
applications for light (color) therapy, but I think you

get the idea. Unfortunately, there still seems to be a lot of resistance to light therapy as a therapeutic approach in western medicine. Perhaps someday that will change.

So, if a "man's life is dyed the color of his imagination," then what color is your life? If it's dull and dreary, then use your imagination to add more color! We see the result of people's imagination everywhere we turn; for example, it's seen in the bodies we carry, the clothes we wear, the homes we live in, the food we eat, the cars we drive, and so on. Let's look at imagination more closely. I would describe it as a thought or creative mental image, but whatever the definition, always remember that our thoughts are energy. Children engage their imagination all the time, but grownups have diminished this natural gift that we were given at birth; unless it involves imagining a lottery win.

Try this exercise. Close your eyes, call in your higher power (B.Y.O.G), clap your hands together ten times, then pull them apart like you are stretching an elastic band; can you feel the energy? Now, image there's a ball of blue light, or any other color between your hands, place them over an achy part on yourself or another person (don't forget to get permission first!); and send love and healing thoughts to that injury. Remove your hands after five-to-ten minutes, shake them out, and thank whom you prayed to for assistance. You can do the same exercise but turn your hands out to the world to send loving and healing energy outward; God knows we need it.

Reflection:

I believe that this chapter of *Fruit Fly Intelligence* offers the most exciting opportunity for you! Even though you may not believe that you can channel Spirit, you know that you have the gift of imagination. With this in mind, I encourage you to spend time reflecting back on the various mental images you have created with your mind; throw in a splash of color to add more depth, see what you can create in your mind, or even manifest into reality: a great book, a new invention, a melody, a perfect solution to a problem, etc. Enjoy!

9

Small Box, Big Messages

*"I believe much trouble would be saved
if we opened our hearts more."*

~ CHIEF JOSEPH (1877–1904)

By December of 2018, my son was off to university and my daughter was living with her dad, so I decided to move into a two-bedroom, two-bathroom condo outfitted with sofa beds to accommodate my grown children whenever they came home. In truth, I believed that I would never find a partner to have a deep romantic relationship with, and therefore, I was preparing to spend the rest of my life on my own. I also felt drawn to a minimalistic lifestyle and downsized my belongings to make this possible; but of course, with Spirit, there is always a reason. I affectionately referred to my condo as *The Intuition Studio,* as a salute to my business, created because of my intuitive journey thus far with Spirit. Initially, the condo was filled with an incredibly peaceful vibe, which my grown children grew to appreciate as much as I did; and I rarely let anyone in to visit our little 1,012-square-foot shoebox because I wanted to keep the energy as pure as possible, or so I thought.

My beloved condo turned out to be a mystical place with a tendency toward the kind of stuff that Sci-Fi films are made of; but this was real! Despite my belief that the condo was filled with a peaceful energy and that Rosepetal was around to protect me, I began to experience malevolent visits from the spirit realm that were way beyond anything I had ever endured before. I placed the print of my white Siberian tiger (Tika) over my bed for added comfort while I slept. Her life-like presence helped me to imagine that all would be well at night. However, I didn't realize until a few years later that I was always safe from physical harm. It's just that those malevolent forces were able to rattle my energetic cage because I had allowed my aura to weaken by overindulging in wine, food, and munchies. Over time, I realized that our body is highly sensitive to energy; therefore, my habits were creating an energetic imbalance, making me more susceptible to psychic attacks. Good to know!

On December 21, 2018, just five days after we moved into the condo, I noticed a sweet little heart on the yellow wall by the balcony door—a gift from

Spirit. I took a picture, and when I expanded the image, I was able to see a second little heart below the obvious one. Remember, I started out as a true skeptic, and admittedly, I wondered if my friends who were doing the condo renovations had secretly painted  the hearts on the wall, but they were just as surprised as I was; and besides, I should know better to even wonder, given the journey I'd had with Spirit. It was an incredible moment indeed, can you see them?!

I continued to experience persistent signs, symbols, and synchronicities, but the ones involving Peter kept our connection and conversations active for several years. Given that he was knee-deep in a personal struggle, it seemed his energetic red wagon was hitched to mine for ongoing support. I was aware of the two cars he owned and began seeing similar makes and models of varying colors driving around town as indications that he was close to me energetically. For example, as I was driving, I would notice two vehicles like his in my rearview mirror—and within the hour, Peter would call or text; it became the hallmark of our etheric connection and the most

reliable sign that he would be contacting me. But
one very peculiar event occurred in the summer of
2018 as I was walking through a parking lot. Everywhere I looked, I saw either one or the other type of
vehicle that Peter drove in various colors. It was eerie
because it made me feel like they were staring at me,
and it turned out to be an ominous sign. A few minutes later, I received a phone call from Peter in sheer
panic! What the heck?!

On September 27, 2018, I decided to ask Spirit
a question about my future husband, since I knew
that it wasn't Peter, and given that I was becoming
increasingly frustrated with our on-again, off-again
relationship. So, I asked Spirit, "When will I meet
my future husband, please?" As I pulled the 2 of
Wands plus the Tower plus the 4 of Swords plus the
6 of Pentacles and sprinkled in some numerology,
I discovered this: $(2 + 16 = 9)$ then, $(4 + 6 = 1)$. I
was able to deduce that an ending was occurring in
my future husband's life. As I finished the reading, I
heard a police car zip by my home. Later, I realized
that this reading referred to the most traumatic experience of my future husband's life!

At the time, I was still connected to Peter, but by
2019, I felt drained by his frequent need of support,
so in that moment I thought it would be best for me

to release myself from this situation; then instantly, I saw his deceased father flash in my mind's eye. He was leaning towards me with his arms up shouting "*Wait, Wait, Wait, Wait, Wait!*" All I could think of was, "are you kidding me right now?!" I understood that Spirit had arranged our mysterious reconnection, but now I could see that his deceased father was in on it too.

For Christmas that year, my children bought me a thoughtful gift that I treasure dearly: two festive coffee mugs. One was labelled "Mr. Claus" and the other was "Mrs. Claus." My kids were fully aware of my deep desire to find love again, one that would last to the end of this lifetime. Along the journey, I continued to meet wonderful men, but no one seemed to have that romantic stickability, and they gave off this energy of "I am not the one!" I found myself balancing the desire to find a love match that would sustain me and the realization that I didn't actually "need" a partner. But there was still something nice about the comfort we ascribe to Mr. and Mrs. Claus' relationship, and the idea was tempting indeed.

Something from Another Dimension

Around January 2020, I experienced something from another dimension that made me feel like I was in a horror movie! The evening began uneventfully when I poured myself a glass of wine and then headed for my comfy couch to watch a period piece movie on Netflix. The first scene of the show was a horrific rape scene of a young girl right in front of her entire family during a home invasion. I gasped and quickly switched to another movie but again was horrified to see the same kind of scene. "Oh my God!" I shouted aloud and immediately asked my Guides for meaning.

That night, I had one of the scariest dreams of my life, and I was completely alone! I had the feeling of being attacked in my sleep, but this wasn't a dream, it turned out to be another psychic attack; made obvious by the events which unfolded over the span of a few days! Given that I had experienced the first one years before, I knew to take them seriously but figured that I would be fine by morning. I must have been in deep REM sleep because my body wouldn't move—the sheer terror of it all kept me paralyzed with fear! I could feel a forceful masculine energy from a small-framed being, short in height, not exactly human, and it was trying to smother me with what looked like a thick, clear plastic face mask. It seemed to have the properties of ectoplasm, which is a thick material that exudes from a medium during a connection with the non-physical realm;[35] anyway, *he* was targeting my mouth! I woke instantly and managed to shake him off. Petrified, I frantically prayed to my Love Team in spirit, requesting immediate and constant protection. I eventually calmed myself enough to fall back to sleep. Would you believe he tried it again that same night! OH MY GOD!

During the day for about a week, I had a very hard time entering my bedroom because of the trauma of it all. I didn't feel that this type of event would kill me, but I felt like *he* was trying to mute me in an attempt to dim my light. I contacted one of my mediumship friends and one of my Reiki teachers for guidance through those frightening experiences because it's common for mystics to encounter negative entities. Whether this was some metaphysical rite of passage or not, I simply had to get ahold of myself! Days passed, and just as I was starting to feel more at ease at bedtime, I was attacked again as I slept; sheer terror came over me once again! I shouted to my Spirit Guides in the darkness, "why is this happening to me?!" I screamed. "I thought you wanted me to help people! How am I supposed to do that with all this *bleep* going on?!" It felt like I had been thrown into an episode of the Twilight Zone![36]

A few days later, I was in the shower getting ready to start my day when I heard my Love Team say that

I was becoming more open to the spirit realm. Some call this a spiritual ascension; and because of it, I could experience more unsavory encounters. What I didn't truly comprehend until years later was that my lousy dietary choices were putting me at risk for such attacks. Here is what I mean, ingesting large quantities of foods of a lower vibrational frequency like processed foods, junk food, excess wine and so forth, and eating without gratitude, had a direct impact on my energy body (aura). It was necessary for me to pay attention to my throat chakra, as this area of my body would begin to play a greater role to fulfill my life purpose; I needed to prepare it for speaking my truth with Spirit through *Fruit Fly Intelligence*. Upon further reflection, I found it fascinating that the very region being attacked was the area of my body that I have wrestled with for most of my life; and the location where I am meant to shine my light. I have been a slave to my palate despite years of attempts to achieve the art of moderation—simply put, I love my food and vino!

During that traumatic week, I also had something wonderful happen. Spirit felt it was time for me to be introduced to another Spirit Guide, one who could be called upon to act as an energetic gatekeeper and protector from negative entities. I already had three gatekeepers (Rosepetal, Tika, and Tyan the black panther) who surrounded me and worked to thwart attacks from lower vibrational forces, but with all this happening, I could certainly use one more! They helped me learn to stand in my power as my channeling skills advanced.

If you are interested in connecting with the supernatural realm or if you are becoming open to a telepathic connection with Spirit, I have good news to share! We have various spiritual beings around us all the time, a posse, if you will. There are Archangels, Angels, Spirit Guides, Soul Guides, Ancestors, Galactic members, and more who help us through certain parts of our journey, while others may be around until the end of this lifetime, and even several lifetimes; no matter what form you take on. Therefore, I encourage you to call upon them whenever you feel the need for protection and guidance.

While in the shower one day where I often spoke with my Love Team in spirit, I thought I'd heard the words "Chief Sancha," and I asked them, "who is that?" In a flash, I bolted out of the shower to get dressed and rushed straight to my computer for answers. I pulled up good ole Google to search the name. Nothing came up. Then I saw a name on the right side of the screen and shouted, "Chief Satanta? Look at the spelling!" Instantly, I felt something land on my left hand; I looked down quickly and saw a sweet little fruit fly! Oh, thank God for this little guy, I thought! That wee little bug's presence confirmed that I was heard, I was safe, and I was meant to meet this Spirit Guide. Chief Satanta, also known as White Bear, was born in either the Kansas or Oklahoma area in 1819, and he spent his life battling for land rights in the face of American colonization efforts. Jailed for murdering American settlers as retribution for the massacre of his own people, he eventually committed suicide on October 11, 1878.[37]

With the Chief looking over my shoulder, I was able to sleep peacefully; the terrorizing events had ceased. At that time, my bedtime routine involved a quick telepathic chat with the Chief whenever I felt something was off to repel nefarious energy. In the beginning of our connection, when I called his name, he would flash his face in front of me and then he'd look up to the Universe; in an instant, I felt safe. To this day, when I refer to him as my new Spirit Guide, he shouts, "I'm not new!"

Another thing you can do to navigate through the etheric realm safely is to imagine that you are protected by visualizing what feels right for you, such as being encapsulated by the white light of Source energy or envisioning yourself in a protective enclosure such as a cocoon, an egg, a bubble, or even a rocket ship—it just depends on where you are and where you're headed; you can call upon Chief Satanta as well for protection. Thank you, Chief!

Fortunately, shadowy experiences, whether physical, emotional, mental, or spiritual, always have a purpose. Do your best to zoom out and observe what's going on around you to find its meaning; for me, it was time for added protection and the privilege to meet the Chief.

Despite the strange goings-on, I settled into life and found it far more peaceful and enjoyable; I attribute this to Spirit and the beautiful people who have entered my life over the last decade or so. I continued to do readings for clients, which still takes my breath away every single time: here is another very kind testimonial from a session in July 2020:

My experience with Paula was amazingly accurate, insightful, compassionate, and truly healing. She has the astounding ability to connect you with your loved ones who have passed over. The precision and validity of her readings is nothing short of stunning. Paula's gift left me speechless as she was able to connect

*with my loved ones with ease. Immediately, I knew
the connection was real and accurate. Names (who
would know about my Uncle Stanley?!), phrases and
very specific details just flow…things a stranger could
not ever know about my family. Paula's language and
words were those of my mother right down to the pet
names she would call us kids. My mom's humour and
strong personality [were] evident throughout the entire session as she spoke to me of things that were privy
and private to only 'my' life. The details were extremely personal. The experience left me emotional and incredibly grateful to have met this amazing woman
who is a conduit of such healing. She is a gift to us all.
Thank you, Paula. You are just extraordinary!*

— *M. K. (Ontario, Canada)*

I had a discussion with this same woman on another occasion; she proceeded to share that her sister,
who was not at all spiritual, found eight dimes lying
around shortly after their mother's death. I mentioned that the number eight on its side represents
the infinity symbol. The *moment* I finished my statement, I felt a needle prick in my left upper back! So,
I asked my client, why did I just get a needle prick in
my back?! She said, "I didn't tell you this Paula, but
even though my mom was in her seventies, she had

a tattoo of the infinity symbol on her back!" It was mind-blowing! And I thought, OMG Spirit, you are *g–o–o–d*!

Energetic Entanglement

Around this time, I got more entangled energetically into the perpetual drama unfolding in Peter's personal life. On July 3, 2020, around 10:30 p.m. I rolled over to go to sleep when, suddenly, I started to have palpitations in my chest, which was very unusual for me. So, I turned onto my right side, but the palpitations continued. What the heck was going on? I ran through the usual culprits that could have brought it on, but I'd had an uneventful day and the same amount of caffeine as usual. About thirty minutes later, I heard a text come through in the darkness, but by then, I was finally feeling a little more settled and chose to ignore my palpitations and the text. The phone rang around 11:00 p.m. It was Peter! He apologized for calling so late but said he desperately needed to talk and was on his way over. I was so confused because he had never called at that time before, and I wondered what the heck was happening here?!

When he finally arrived at the door, I looked past him into the night sky and noticed that we met under the Capricorn full moon, which had been enveloped by the colors of the rainbow; it was spectacular! As I was showing him in, Spirit nudged me to put two and two together; that is the moment when I knew for certain that Spirit had entangled our hearts energetically to ensure our lessons would be learned. But on this night, my palpitations reflected his stressed heart. It was head-scratching and jaw-dropping all at the same time. How could this be? How could my body be feeling another person's troubles? What I realized was that my physical heart was signaling a problem with Peter's heart-wrenching emotions, made possible through our interconnection with Spirit; and my heart was absolutely fine! My focus in those moments turned to my friend's need to vent while I sat and listened, and then I offered my intuitive support through a very tumultuous situation that beat him down from every angle. Even though he was struggling in ways that I just couldn't understand, I had to accept my role as a friend and intuitive advisor, and I continued to provide unconditional love to help him through.

From one bizarre event to another! At some point while living in the condo, I had two pleasant, yet fleeting encounters with aliens. I find it odd that I don't have those dates solidified in my mind, but

I suppose that dates are unimportant in this case. Anyway, the first came through my mind's eye as I was drifting off to sleep. If you imagine an old TV screen, picture the alien coming from the bottom of the frame, like a PowerPoint animation, gliding into the center of the box. *He* was bluish in color with an elongated head, wide saucer type eyes that were dark and lacked the pupils and irises of human eyes. His shoulders were pronounced, emphasizing his small frame. He looked right at me! I knew he knew that I could see him; the energy was benevolent and ancestral in nature; there was no message other than that they are here among us; I knew he was an advanced expression of Source energy.

The second experience occurred in the middle of the night. I awoke and was about to drag my sleepy body to the bathroom when, suddenly, I saw three aliens at the bottom right corner of my bed! They appeared holographic with a green hue and looked like they were the same or similar species as my other visitor. They were actively moving downward and thankfully toward the other direction, as if taking an escalator to another floor. Needless to say, my bladder had to wait! None of these four aliens were robotic, nor were they an artificial intelligence, instead, they seemed to have a consciousness; I suspect that I will have more benevolent encounters in the future. After these unbelievable experiences, I made a conscious decision to ignore my doubts and became even more open to the journey my Guides were taking me on. I began to fully accept that everything happens for a reason and learned to sit back, relax, and enjoy the show as Spirit continued to bring more amazing people, places, and things onto my path.

Reflection:

Whoa! I opened my heart to Spirit, and look what flowed in: more hearts, a scheming loved one (Peter's dad); more psychic invaders; a not-so-new gatekeeper, thank God; another fruit fly; more readings; more pokes from Spirit; more broken hearts; all for more lessons! Stop the train, I'm getting off! Well, after the next stop.

10

New Home, New Life

"Only by joy and sorrow does a person know anything
about themselves and their destiny. They learn
what to do and what to avoid."

~ JOHANN WOLFGANG VON GOETHE (1749–1832)

In early February 2021, Peter had contacted me
again, only this time, he sounded weaker than before. I found myself sitting and listening once again
to a situation in his home life that had gone from bad
to worse. This was the moment when I decided that I
had no more to give to help him through. I felt completely deflated from the over-giving and under-re-
ceiving cycle we'd been locked into; and by then, my
spiritual lessons had been learned. But before we
said goodbye, he asked, "how do I go forward?" We
paused, and then the words fell out of my mouth:
"Just channel my energy when you need strength." I
trusted that my spiritual gatekeepers would continue
to regulate access to me and understood that it was
the right help to offer him in that moment. With

that, I knew our time was done, but not without a finale performance by two cars that resembled his. You're not going to believe this, but as I was driving on the highway one day around this time, I saw an SUV like his, in his color. It pulled in front of me and seconds later, a fancy car, also in his color, pulled up behind me, and in that very moment, a song we enjoyed played on the radio! After it was over, the cars drove away in unison, signaling the end of this car synchronicity with Peter. It left me dumbfounded! True freaking story!

I can sum it all up to say that my interconnection between *Spirit, Peter, and me* led to:

- a refinement in my ability to channel
- an understanding that deceased loved ones can assist to bring people together
- the knowledge that our body can become entangled energetically with others, which can impact our body's performance
- that energetic entanglements can occur with inanimate objects, as it did with Peter's cars, and
- the big takeaway for me is that Spirit can channel through everything.

For Peter, I understood that he needed to feel love, of the purest kind; connecting the sex organs is one thing (Root Chakra), but loving from the heart space (Heart Chakra) literally happens on a whole other level. Our connection would be the opportunity for him to feel loved in order to find self-love, after being tangled in a parasitic co-dependent relationship that he'd been planning to leave for years prior to our reacquaintance. However, Peter's wake-up call to put himself first occurred about a year later through a bout with cancer and chemo from "Hell." Peter had been whittled down to a shell of a man as his physical body had taken the brunt of years of emotional turmoil.

Once his cancer was in remission, he took action and left the toxic situation behind, which apparently had worsened over time; I congratulated him and wished him well on his journey, knowing that our bond would remain in Divine custody. I closed that door with Peter for good, but as they say, when one door closes, another one opens, and indeed it did! The very next day, I received some positive news about something I had proposed at work, and by the nineteenth of February of that year, my wish to be moved to a permanent part-time position was granted. It is noteworthy that a part-time role is quite uncommon in the industry that I work in, and yet it happened! I have my two wonderful former bosses to thank for that, along with Spirit, of course, and I couldn't be more grateful! Remember that miracles can and do happen with Spirit, all you have to do is ask.

Fortunately, the wave of good luck didn't end there. I decided to join an online dating site and wasn't having much luck in my search. I got an inkling to cast a wider net, as I checked the box to include potential suitors from the United States. The day after I was granted part-time status, and with my Mr. and Mrs. Claus mugs in full view, I asked Spirit, *where is my Mr. Claus?*

Then, lo and behold I received a response from a cutie in Alaska! After several conversations, I started to believe that my knight in shining armor had finally arrived! He was a little battered and bruised, but still intact. As you can imagine, the week we met felt like an enchanting technicolored carpet ride, oh what a feeling! In hindsight, I was able to piece together the plethora of signs, symbols, and synchronicities that had played out prior to his arrival on that fateful day. I instinctively knew that we had manifested this connection with Spirit's help of course; only this time, I wasn't required to become lockstepped and was therefore freer to determine the outcome.

Cue the flurry of signs, symbols, and synchronicities that appeared through the years leading up to my future husband's arrival. About five years prior to meeting him, I had been seeing the letter "K" all over the place, in the usual pop-art-like fashion: at gas stations, on trucks, t-shirts, mud flaps, merchandise, and words normally spelled with a "C" took on this new trend of being spelled with a "K" instead. I figured that Spirit would eventually let me know if it had significance for my life, and sure enough, it did; it was a foreshadowing of who was on his way in! Looking back, I also saw the number "5" everywhere and recall joking about having nightmares of the number 5 chasing me down the street; that turned out to have meaning, too, without the nightmare part.

And guess what? His name is Kris, not Christopher, not Christian, just Kris, so I playfully dubbed him my Kris Kringle right out the gate (AKA Mr. Claus)! Our whirlwind romance began, thanks to WhatsApp. The banter was out of this world, and soon we would address each other by our last names. As we learned more about one another, I found out that the tarot reading I had done on September 27, 2018, was unbelievably accurate!

Mending a Broken Heart

During the fall of 2018, when Kris was still a complete mystery to me, he would go through the most painful experience of his life; on October 7, 2018, while he was away at work, his beloved wife passed unexpectedly in her sleep. During the next two-and-a-half years, he'd be busy mending his broken heart, as I was being schooled by Spirit. There were many subtle signs, starting with that sweet letter K which obviously turned out to have meaning, given his first name of course. Also, the number 5 was extremely important, as it represented the future number of members in my core family with Kris, Radley (his fur baby), my two beautiful children, and me. Kris told me that Radley's breed is a blue heeler; I chuckled and said I'm a blue healer too, with tongue in cheek.

But one thing that caught me off guard was seeing his wife in spirit as she brought her two index fingers together, indicating that she had assisted in my coming together with Kris. Additionally, I had received a fascinating vision as I was drifting off to sleep. In a flash, Spirit gave me a glimpse into a past life when Kris and I were together, although I have since been told that he spent much of his time searching for me back then. In this vision, he was dressed in a white toga laced with Greek energy and came with a knowing that he *is* the one that I will marry in this lifetime. It is interesting to note that my mother calls him Kristo, apparently, Kristo is a baby boy name of Latin origin. Similar to the Greek name Christopher, Kristo means "follower of Christ" and "bearing Christ."[38] Well, that made sense, too.

Since then, Kris and I have spent months mapping out endless scenarios about how we could make our long-distance relationship work, with him in Alaska, USA, and me in Ontario, Canada, factoring in my grown children and one big loveable dog. After just a few visits to both cities, we realized that my beloved condo was not going to be large enough for the five of us. Even if you meet "the one", it does not preclude you from having to deal with challenges. On the contrary! So, we finally agreed that I would buy a home closer to the border and he would eventually buy one in Arizona where he was born and planned to retire; this meant that we needed to work out the legalities and logistics to come together in whatever form that took. For now, Kris still resides in Alaska.

By April 1, 2022, I listed the condo for sale with my agent and began the painstaking task of completing upgrades, doing incessant cleaning, and stepping out for showings. It took five months to sell, way too long by anyone's standards, I am sure. While I was managing that, I was also dragging Imants along to various cities and home showings to figure out where I would find the most suitable home for Kris and my family to live, while factoring in my future grandchildren as well; the search also took about five months to complete. I had asked my Spirit Guides to assist in finding me the perfect home, and with that I'd have to say, be careful what you wish for!

The first home I fell for was ripe with spiritual energy, made obvious by the orb I saw in one of the real estate photographs online. I fell hard for this beautiful old home, which had been built in 1875; it came with a garage that had been converted from a carriage house for horses into a space for cars. Given my journey with Spirit, I was newly drawn to century-old homes. However, a few nights later as I was deep in sleep, I awoke suddenly gasping in sheer terror as my sleepy eyes glanced toward the left of the bed where a tall figure stood wearing a medieval-like black cloak with an oversized hood covering the head. Fortunately, I couldn't see the face, but it felt male, and with that, the message was load and clear! This home would not be suitable for us energetically!

I continued with my search for the perfect home, and after several lunch bag letdowns, I found a lovely old farmhouse built in 1862 that was filled with character and equipped with modern-day amenities. I had the pleasure of visiting, but just as I dove in for more information, it was plucked off the market. Unbelievable! I carried on with the search but couldn't get this lovely old home out of my head, so I decided to pull up in front of the house with the intention of leaving the owner a note expressing my interest. But as I looked up, I saw three women wearing the same red team-like t-shirt leaning forward and staring right at me; for me it was a sign that there would be issues with people if I bought this incredible home. Sure enough, I found out later that there was an unresolved issue with neighbors involving a shared fence. Wow, barriers can make great protectors!

So, of course, the journey to find our home continued, and just like the story of Goldilocks and the Three Bears, the last home I fell for was just right! This charming little home was built in 1917 and has an addition that gives it a cozy Cape Cod feel; it was enveloped with an ancestral presence, and with that, we moved in on November 3rd, 2022. Within the first four months, I had already experienced a number of bizarre supernatural events; here is what has happened so far.

Celebrating a Soulful Marriage

On January 10, 2023, Kris and I finally shared a soulful marriage in Hawaii with loved ones by our side, almost two years after our connection began. But on February 5th, 2023, while headed to Arizona for our honeymoon, Spirit would make an appearance about 30,000 feet in the air. I was in the airplane lavatory when two orbs zipped past my right periphery; I said, "Hi Spirit, fancy meeting you here," and chuckled. Well, it turned out to be a signal for what was coming next, as I later leaned into a conversation with a guy sitting in the window seat next to me. After a quick exchange and mention of my mediumship work, I shared that I was hoping to launch a book on April 27th (better late than never). Well, the passenger's eyes bulged out of his head because his deceased brother shared the same birthdate as me. Then his brother showed up in spirit and offered a few signature tidbits which left this guy completely in shock: it's never a dull moment with Spirit!

Another fascinating moment occurred in our new home when I called upon the previous deceased homeowners collectively in spirit: right after

PAULA MARUCCI

I finished my sentence, two orbs flew by—oh my goodness, it was like orbs-on-demand! And another thing, I was thanking the deceased owners and families for their loving energy when all of a sudden, a light went off and back on in a flash! My heart raced because I knew they had heard me, and it freaked me out just the same. Anyway, it was at that time when we became heavily involved in home renovations, and I was thrilled to learn that there were no mouse droppings behind the walls, which is incredibly impressive given the age of our home; but of course, there were a few spiders hanging around, no surprise, right?! I found two big black spiders, like the one that had been sitting on the back of my pink housecoat long ago. So, I told them aloud, "okay guys, you know you gotta 'go-go' outside!" I sounded like I was herding cats, but I just couldn't chance them settling into my boots or making themselves comfortable in my jammies. Luckily, we were having unseasonably warm weather, so placing them outdoors was fine.

In February 2023, as heavy snow and freezing rain blanketed the ground, I stumbled onto the same type of spider sitting on the basement stairs and so I said to it, "I'm not sure you will make it in this weather, but you gotta 'go-go' outside!" Days later, as I was resting in bed after doing some readings for clients, I looked up and saw the same spider energetically, only his energy was as big as a mid-sized dog. He came charging into my bedroom, lifted his front leg and smacked me across the face! I was shocked and began laughing at what had just taken place; however, the next day I found his poor lifeless body lying on the porch and instantly understood the reason for the slap and felt bad for causing him grief.

I will share one last experience that has randomly recurred over the years since my intuitive journey kicked up; it was on March 1, 2023, when I washed up and got settled into bed. As I lay down and shut my eyes, I immediately became wide-eyed with fear, because this foreign sensation that seemed so benign was making its presence known. The best way I can describe it, is it feels like a head-to-toe quiver from a whack to the funny bone. In the back of my mind, I wondered if it was the alien who visited years ago. I was completely freaked out because it was the strongest one yet and seemed more celestial than before. I chose not to ask my Guides about the cause, because I might never sleep again! But I got a sense that my energy was being tweaked to get me ready for the next chapter to begin. With that in mind, I called upon my gatekeepers, thanked them, rolled over, and fell asleep.

Reflection:

Like Johann Wolfgang von Goethe and you dear reader, I have had a life filled with joy and sorrow too, with a dash of crazy thrown in! But the last seventeen years have been extraordinary indeed because it taught me about my life purpose, which has been aptly designed to serve you.

Acknowledgements

Fruit Fly Intelligence could not have materialized into the physical realm without the love and ongoing support of my entire Love Team in spirit; comprised of my Guardian Angels, Spirit Guides, Soul Guides, Ancestors, and beloved spiritual gatekeepers—Rosepetal, Tika, Chief Satanta, and Tyan; my orb family and fruit fly friends, as they continue to show up for me. This chapter of my life has been filled with countless spiritual lessons that have left me frazzled and bewildered way too often, but now that it's over, I feel more like myself than ever before; it's over, right?! But seriously, I thank you with all that I am; because of you, I am home.

To my interconnected soul friends, I thank you for the honor of accompanying me in this lifetime; the wallops and gobsmacks have helped me to grow. It is said that good things come to those who wait, but I would modify it to say, good things come to those who learn.

And to those who validated my words, without you I would not have believed in myself, nor my ability to channel the invisible realm. Your outpouring of love and support provided the momentum I needed to share my inner world with all of you.

To my beautiful mother, Lynda. Thank you for sharing innumerable hours with me, listening, supporting, advising, and cooking incredible food for my belly; You are a gift to us all. Love you Mom!

To my gorgeous children, Thomas and Caroline; I am sorry our journey wasn't easier, but we finally made it, and I couldn't be prouder of you! I love you all the way to the moon and back!

To my brother Stephen, my sister Rhonda and our family, there is nothing like sharing good food and laugher, keep it coming! I love you guys. And Dad, I love you too.

To Imants: A jack of all trades, and a master of pretty much all of them! Thank you for showing up tirelessly and supporting me on the earth plane; you are truly one of a kind; thank you for sharing your light with us!

To my dear friends Daniela, Shelly, Meena, Ian, Ivars, Dani, Rachael, Lovey, Emmanuel, Rebecca, Chelsea, and Karen for helping me keep my feet on the ground while the supernatural became super challenging; I love you. To my mediumship sisters: Donna, Sharon, and Sarah: thank you for illuminating my path.

To Dr. John: Thank you for lending your hip and being open to what came next; and for taking it seriously as a doctor. Also, thank you so much for taking the time to write the *Foreword* of this book, sharing your unique perspective as a cardiac surgeon is precisely what Spirit had planned.

To Corey Poirier: Thank you for your willingness to review *Fruit Fly Intelligence*; hope it was more thrilling than you could have imagined!

To my incredible editor, author Susan Crossman: Thank you for sharing your wisdom, skills, connections, and wit; I knew from our initial exchange that my book baby would be in good hands.

To my graphic designer, Kelly Pasholk: Thank you for your patience and creative ideas; you have been an absolute joy to work with.

To my proofreader, Susan Gaigher: Thank you for working meticulously to ensure that my book would be worthy of its readers.

To the beta reader team, Lindsay Millburn, Michael Ring, and Rasche Subritzski: Thank you for your time and willingness to help *Fruit Fly Intelligence* be the best it can be.

To Kris: Thank you for showing up in Divine timing; being ready and able to roll up your sleeves for the biggest adventure yet. I love you.

To Masaru Emoto (AKA Emoto-san): Thank you for giving water a voice in your book titled; *The Hidden*

Messages in Water. Indeed, we are all connected. To Prime Source Energy: Thank you and I love you.

I love you all, thank you.

Bibliography

Adrienne, Carol. *The Purpose of Your Life*. New York, NY: Eagle Brook Publishing, 1998.

Alexander, Eben. *Proof Of Heaven*. New York, NY: Simon & Schuster Paperbacks, 2012.

American Museum of Natural History. "The Color of Light." Accessed October 10, 2023. https://www.amnh.org/explore/ology/physics/see-the-light2/the-color-of-light#:~:text=The%20light%20that%20we%20see,still%20many%20variations%20of%20wavelengths.

AZ Animals. "Fruit Fly Drosophila melanogaster." April 8, 2022. https://a-z-animals.com/animals/fruit-fly/.

Baron-Reid, Colette. *Remembering the Future*. Carlsbad, California: Hay House, Inc., 2006.

Berres, Janet. *Your Guide to the Tarot*. Woodbury, Minnesota: Llewellyn Publications, 2005.

Braden, Gregg. *The Spontaneous Healing of Belief*. Carlsbad, California: Hay House, Inc., 2009.

Britannica. "History & Society: ectoplasm." October 3, 2023. https://www.britannica.com/topic/ectoplasm-occultism.

Britannica. "Science & Tech: electron." Accessed October 10, 2023. https://www.britannica.com/science/electron.

Britannica "Science & Tech: telepathy." September 28, 2023. https://www.britannica.com/topic/telepathy.

Britannica. "The Britannica Dictionary: transmitter." Accessed October 11, 2023. https://www.britannica.com/dictionary/transmitter.

Britannica. "Science & Tech: vibration." Accessed October 10, 2023. https://www.britannica.com/science/vibration.

British Museum. "Marie-Anne-Adélaïde Lenormand." Accessed October 9, 2023. https://www.britishmuseum.org/collection/term/BIOG182148.

Browne, Sylvia. *Contacting Your Spirit Guide*. Carlsbad, California: Hay House, Inc., 2005.

Bryan, Charles S, T. Jock Murray, Mark E Silverman, eds. "The Quotable Osler." *Journal of the Royal Society of Medicine*. https://www.ncbi.nlm.nih.gov/pmc/articles/PMC539583/. Accessed November 19, 2023.

Byrne, Lorna. *Angels In My Hair*. New York, NY: Three Rivers Press, 2008.

Byrne, Rhonda. *The Secret*. New York, NY: Beyond Words Publishing, 2006.

Cambridge Dictionary. "Synchronicity." Accessed October 9, 2023. https://dictionary.cambridge.org/dictionary/english/synchronicity.

Choquette, Sonia. *Trust Your Vibes*. Carlsbad, California: Hay House, Inc., 2004.

Clayton, Victoria. "What Is Reiki And How Does It Work?" *Forbes Health*, September 1, 2023. https://www.forbes.com/health/body/what-is-reiki/.

Cleveland Clinic. "LED Light Therapy." December 2, 2021. https://my.clevelandclinic.org/health/treatments/22146-led-light-therapy.

Coelho, Paulo. *The Alchemist*. New York, NY: HarperCollins Publishers, Inc,. 1993.

Comprehensive Guide to The Wonderful World of Psychology. "Old Woman Young Woman Illusion" All-About-Psychology.com. Accessed October 10, 2023. https://www.all-about-psychology.com/old-woman-young-woman-illusion.html#:~:text=The%20famous%20Old%20Woman%20Young,in%20Puck%20magazine%20in%201915.

Desai, Mary-Anne. "Baby Names: Kristo." The Bump, April 10, 2023. https://www.thebump.com/b/kristo-baby-name.

Dispenza, Joe. *Becoming Supernatural*. Carlsbad, California: Hay House, Inc., 2017.

Dyer, Wayne. *The Power of Intention*. Carlsbad, California: Hay House, Inc., 2005.

Emoto, Masaru. *The Hidden Messages in Water.* Hillsboro, OR: Beyond Words Publishing, Inc., 2004.

Fluke. "What is Frequency?" Accessed October 10, 2023. https://www.fluke.com/en-ca/learn/blog/electrical/what-is-frequency.

Frankl, Viktor E. *Man's Search For Meaning.* Boston, Massachusetts: Beacon Press, 2017.

Frederick, Sue. *I See Your Dream Job.* New York, NY: St. Martin's Griffin Edition, 2010.

Goldsmith, Charlie. "Feasibility of Energy Medicine in a Community Teaching Hospital: An Exploratory Case Series." Charlie Goldsmith, June 3, 2015. https://www.charliegoldsmith.com/studies.

Grace, Raymon. *The Future Is Yours.* Charlottesville, VA: Hampton Roads Publishing Company, Inc., 2014.

Guinness World Records. "Roger Bannister: First sub-four-minute mile." Accessed October 8, 2023. https://www.guinnessworldrecords.com/records/hall-of-fame/first-sub-four-minute-mile.

Health & Bass. "Frequencies + The Body." August 20, 2021. https://www.healthandbass.com/post/frequencies-and-the-body.

HealthLink BC. "Light Therapy." June 16, 2021, https://www.healthlinkbc.ca/health-topics/light-therapy#:~:text=Light%20therapy%20is%20an%20effective,improve%20in%20the%20second%20week.

Heartmath Institute. "Science of the Heart." Accessed October 10, 2023. https://www.heartmath.org/research/science-of-the-heart/energetic-communication/#:~:text=The%20heart%20is%20the%20most,activity%20generated%20by%20the%20brain.

Hicks, Esther and Jerry. *Ask and It Is Given.* Carlsbad, California: Hay House, Inc., 2004.

Holland, John. *Power of the Soul.* Carlsbad, California: Hay House, Inc., 2007.

Johnson, Spencer. *The Present.* New York City, NY: Doubleday Publishing, 2003.

Katz, Markus and Tali Goodwin. *Easy Lenormand Handbook.* Woodbury, Minnesota: Llewellyn Publications, 2015.

Katz, Markus and Tali Goodwin. *Fairy Lenormand Oracle Cards.* Torino, Italy: Lo Scarabeo, 2015.

Kiel, Anysia. *Discovering the Medium Within.* Woodbury, Minnesota: Llewellyn Publications, 2013.

Kiger, Patrick J. "8 Facts About Ancient Egypt's Hieroglyphic Writing." History. July 25, 2023. https://www.history.com/news/hieroglyphics-facts-ancient-egypt.

Madeleine L'Engle, *A Wrinkle in Time*, (New York: Square Fish, 2007), 46.

May, Jon D. "The Encyclopedia of Oklahoma History and Culture: SATANTA (ca. 1819–1878)." Oklahoma Historical Society. Accessed October 12, 2023. https://www.okhistory.org/publications/enc/entry.php?entry=SA024.

McCants, Glynis. *Glynis Has Your Number.* New York, NY: The Numbers Lady, Inc., 2005.

Merriam-Webster Dictionary. "Cartomancy." Accessed October 9, 2023. https://www.merriam-webster.com/dictionary/cartomancy.

Moore, Thomas. *Care of the Soul.* New York, NY: HarperCollins Publishers, Inc,. 1992.

Murphy, Joseph. *The Power of Your Subconscious Mind.* Mansfield Centre, CT: Martino Publishing, 2011.

Myss, Caroline. "Chakras – Your Energetic Being." Accessed October 8, 2023. https://www.myss.com/chakras/.

Myss, Caroline. *Sacred Contracts.* New York, NY: Harmony Books, 2001.

National Geographic. "Y2K bug." Accessed October 8, 2023. https://education.nationalgeographic.org/resource/Y2K-bug/.

National Library of Medicine. "The Quotable Osler." Journal of the Royal Society of Medicine. Accessed November 19, 2023. https://www.ncbi.nlm.nih.gov/pmc/articles/PMC539583/#:~:text=He%20believed%20'that%20the%20practice,admired%20by%20students%20and%20colleagues.

Neal, Mary C. *To Heaven and Back.* Colorado Springs, Colorado: WaterBrook Press, 2012.

Oates, Barb. "'The Healer': Charlie Goldsmith on His Special Gift and New TLC Series." TV Insider, accessed October 31, 2023. https://www.tvinsider.com/648345/meet-charlie-goldsmith-of-tlcs-the-healer/.

Orloff, Judith. *Guide to Intuitive Healing.* Three Rivers Press, 2000.

Plante, Amber. "How the human body uses electricity." University of Maryland Graduate School. Accessed October 10, 2023. https://www.graduate.umaryland.edu/gsa/gazette/February-2016/How-the-human-body-uses-electricity/#:~:text=Electricity%20is%20everywhere%2C%20even%20in,to%20move%2C%20think%20and%20feel.

Redfield, James. *The Celestine Prophecy.* New York, NY: Warner Books, Inc., 1993.

Rosen, Rebecca. "Intuition 101: Developing Your Clairsenses." Oprah.com, June 11, 2010. https://www.oprah.com/spirit/intuition-101-developing-your-clairsenses/all.

Schulz, Charles M. "Pig-Pen." Peanuts.com, accessed October 31, 2023. https://www.peanuts.com/about/pigpen.

Serling, Rod. "The Twilight Zone." Onondaga Historical Association, accessed October 31, 2023. https://www.cnyhistory.org/2014/12/rod-serling/#:~:text=On%20this%20day%20in%201924,Awards%2C%20and%20a%20Golden%20Globe.

Shine, Betty. *Mind Waves: The Ultimate Energy that Could Change the World.* Great Britain: Bantam Press, 1993.

Space.com. "The double-slit experiment: Is light a wave or a particle?" Accessed October 23, 2024. https://www.space.com/double-slit-experiment-light-wave-or-particle.

Stanborough, Rebecca Joy. "What Is Vibrational Energy?" Healthline. November 13, 2020. https://www.healthline. com/health/vibrational-energy.

STEM Generation. "Potato Power!" Accessed October 10, 2023. https://stemgeneration.org/potato-power/#:~:text=The%20potato%20battery%20is%20a,an%20 LED%20light%20or%20clock.

Thibodeau, Lauren. *Natural Born Intuition*. Franklin Lakes, NJ: The Career Press, Inc., 2005.

Tyson, Neil deGrasse. *Astrophysics for People in a Hurry*. New York, NY: W. W. Norton & Company, 2017.

United States Department of Defense. "Statement by the Department of Defense on the Release of Historical Navy Videos." April 27, 2020. https://www.defense.gov/News/ Releases/Release/Article/2165713/statement-by-the-department-of-defense-on-the-release-of-historical-navy-videos/.

University Corporation for Atmospheric Research. "Wavelength of Blue and Red Light." Accessed October 10, 2023. https://scied.ucar.edu/image/wavelength-blue-and-red-light-image#:~:text=Blue%20light%20has%20a%20 higher,more%20energy%20than%20red%20light.

University of Missouri-Columbia. "Sex-deprived fruit flies turn to alcohol, perhaps to fulfill a physiological demand for a reward." ScienceDaily. Accessed October 8, 2023.https:// www.sciencedaily.com/releases/2012/03/120315145415.htm.

Virtue, Doreen, and Robert Reeves. *Nutrition for Intuition*. Carlsbad, California: Hay House, Inc., 2016.

Wisconsin Historical Society. "Mary Hayes-Chynoweth, Psychic Healer." Accessed October 8, 2023. https://www. wisconsinhistory.org/Records/Article/CS309.

Zukav, Gary. *Soul Stories*. New York, NY: Simon & Schuster, 2000.

Endnotes

1 Masaru Emoto, The Hidden Messages in Water (Hillsboro: Beyond Words Publishing, Inc., 2004), 5.

2 "Sex-deprived fruit flies turn to alcohol, perhaps to fulfill a physiological demand for a reward," Science Daily March 2015), https://www.sciencedaily.com/releases/2012/03/120315145415.htm#:~:text=Summary%3A,could%20help%20treat%20human%20addictions.

3 "Roger Bannister: First sub-four-minute mile," Guinness World Records, accessed October 9, 2023, https://www.guinnessworldrecords.com/records/hall-of-fame/first-sub-four-minute-mile.

4 "Mary Hayes-Chynoweth, Psychic Healer," Wisconsin Historical Society, accessed October 8, 2023, https://www.wisconsinhistory.org/Records/Article/CS309.

5 "Y2K bug," National Geographic, accessed October 8, 2023, https://education.nationalgeographic.org/resource/Y2K-bug/.

6 Caroline Myss, "Chakras – Your Energetic Being," Caroline Myss, accessedOctober 8, 2023, https://www.myss.com/chakras/.

7 "Statement by the Department of Defense on the Release of Historical Navy Videos," U.S. Department of Defense, April 27, 2020, https://www.defense.gov/News/Releases/Release/Article/2165713/statement-by-the-department-of-defense-on-the-release-of-historical-navy-videos/.

8 "Synchronicity," Cambridge Dictionary, accessed October 9, 2023, https://dictionary.cambridge.org/dictionary/english/synchronicity.

9 Markus Katz and Tali Goodwin, Fairy Lenormand Oracle Cards (Torino: Lo Scarabeo, 2015), 7.

10 "Cartomancy," Merriam-Webster Dictionary, accessed October 9, 2023, https://www.merriam-webster.com/dictionary/cartomancy.

11 "Marie-Anne-Adélaïde Lenormand," The British Museum, accessed October 9, 2023, https://www.britishmuseum.org/collection/term/BIOG182148.

12 Patrick J. Kiger, "8 Facts About Ancient Egypt's Hieroglyphic Writing," History, July 25, 2023, https://www.history.com/news/hieroglyphics-facts-ancient-egypt.

13 Rebecca Rosen, "Intuition 101: Developing Your Clairsenses," Oprah.com, June 11, 2020, https://www.oprah.com/spirit/intuition-101-developing-your-clairsenses/all.

14 "Science & Tech: telepathy," Britannica, September 28, 2023, https://www.britannica.com/topic/telepathy.

15 "A Comprehensive Guide To The Wonderful World of Psychology," All-About-Psychology.com, accessed October 10, 2023, https://www.all-about-psychology.com/old-woman-young-woman-illusion.html#:~:text=The%20famous%20Old%20Woman%20Young,in%20Puck%20magazine%20in%201915.

16 "Science & Tech: electron," Britannica, accessed October 10, 2023, https://www.britannica.com/science/electron.

17 "Potato Power!," STEM Generation, accessed October 10, 2023, https://stemgeneration.org/potato-power/#:~:text=The%20potato%20battery%20is%20a,an%20LED%20light%20or%20clock.

18 Amber Plante, "How the human body uses electricity," University of Maryland, accessed October 10, 2023, https://www.graduate.umaryland.edu/gsa/gazette/February-2016/How-the-human-body-uses-electricity/#:~:text=Electricity%20is%20everywhere%2C%20even%20in,to%20move%2C%20think%20and%20feel.

19 "Science of the Heart," Heartmath Institute, accessed October 10, 2023, https://www.heartmath.org/research/science-of-the-heart/energetic-communication/#:~:text=The%20heart%20is%20the%20most,activity%20generated%20by%20the%20brain.

20 Charles M. Schultz, "Pig-Pen," Peanuts.com, accessed October 31, 2023, https://www.peanuts.com/about/pigpen.

21 "The double-slit experiment: Is light a wave or a particle?" Space.com, accessed October 10, 2023, https://www.space.com/double-slit-experiment-light-wave-or-particle.

22 "The Color of Light," American Museum of Natural History, accessed October 10, 2023, https://www.amnh.org/explore/ology/physics/see-the-light2/the-color-of-light#:~:text=The%20light%20that%20we%20see,still%20many%20variations%20of%20wavelengths.

23 "Wavelength of Blue and Red Light," University Corporation for Atmospheric Research, accessed October 10, 2023, https://scied.ucar.edu/image/wavelength-blue-and-red-light-image#:~:text=Blue%20light%20has%20a%20higher,more%20energy%20than%20red%20light.

24 "Science & Tech: Vibration," Britannica, accessed October 10, 2023, https://www.britannica.com/science/vibration.

25 Rebecca Joy Stanborough, "What Is Vibrational Energy?" Healthline, November 13,2020, https://www.healthline.com/health/vibrational-energy.

26 "What is Frequency?" Fluke, accessed October 10, 2023, https://www.fluke.com/en-ca/learn/blog/electrical/what-is-frequency.

27 "Frequencies + The Body," Health & Bass, August 20, 2021, https://www.healthandbass.com/post/frequencies-and-the-body.

28 "Fruit Fly: Drosophila melanogaster," AZ Animals, April 8, 2022, https://a-z-animals.com/animals/fruit-fly/.

29 "The Britannica Dictionary: transmitter," Britannica, accessed October 11, 2023, https://www.britannica.com/dictionary/transmitter.

30 Victoria Clayton, "What Is Reiki And How Does It Work?" Forbes Health, September 1, 2023, https://www.forbes.com/health/body/what-is-reiki/.

31 Barb Oates, "'The Healer': Charlie Goldsmith on His Special Gift and New TLC Series," TV Insider, accessed October 31, 2023, https://www.tvinsider.com/648345/meet-charlie-goldsmith-of-tlcs-the-healer/.

32   Charlie Goldsmith, "Feasibility of Energy Medicine in a Community Teaching Hospital: An Exploratory Case Series," Charlie Goldsmith, June 3, 2015, https://www.charliegoldsmith.com/studies.

33 "Light Therapy," British Columbia: HealthLink BC, June 16, 2021, https://www.healthlinkbc.ca/health-topics/light-therapy#:~:text=Light%20therapy%20is%20an%20effective,improve%20in%20the%20second%20week.

34 "LED Light Therapy," Cleveland Clinic, 12/02/2021, https://my.clevelandclinic.org/health/treatments/22146-led-light-therapy.

35 "History & Society: ectoplasm," Britannica, October 3, 2023, https://www.britannica.com/topic/ectoplasm-occultism.

36 Rod Serling, "The Twilight Zone," Onondaga Historical Association, accessed October 31, 2023, https://www.cnyhistory.org/2014/12/rod-serling/#:~:text=On%20this%20day%20in%201924,Awards%2C%20and%20a%20Golden%20Globe.

37 Jon D. May, "The Encyclopedia of Oklahoma History and Culture: SATANTA (ca. 1819–1878)," Oklahoma Historical Society, October 12, 2023, https://www.okhistory.org/publications/enc/entry.php?entry=SA024.

38 Mary-Anne Desai, "Baby Names," The Bump, April 10, 2023, https://www.thebump.com/b/kristo-baby-name.

*Thank you for reading Fruit Fly Intelligence.
I hope you enjoyed my journey and discovered at least
one takeaway to help you live an extraordinary life!*

*If you would like to learn more about your personal
navigating system (PNS), then please contact me at
fruitflyintelligence.com*

About the Author

RITA ZIETSMA PHOTOGRAPHY

Paula Marucci is a psychic medium and energy channeler who began her career as a Registered Nurse; she was educated at the Toronto Metropolitan University and holds a Bachelor of Science in Nursing (BScN). Paula is well sought after for her intuitive guidance given her years of experience with the supernatural realm. She is using her spiritual gift and sharing her wisdom to help others heal and live an extraordinary life! Paula is available for personal readings and motivational speaking engagements; she lives in Ontario, Canada. Her website is fruitflyintelligence.com

Printed in the USA
CPSIA information can be obtained
at www.ICGtesting.com
LVHW020405210824
788814LV00006B/19